THE POWER
TO LEAD

To Lance

Keep powering your
purpose.

M Thomas .

THE POWER TO LEAD

HOW TO OPTIMIZE YOUR ENERGY TO THRIVE IN LEADERSHIP

Marisa Thomas

gatekeeper press™

Tampa, Florida

The Power to Lead: How to Optimize Your Energy to Thrive in Leadership

Published by Gatekeeper Press
7853 Gunn Hwy., Suite 209
Tampa, FL 33626
www.GatekeeperPress.com

Illustration by Taina Layla Cunion

Library of Congress Control Number: 2023950742

ISBN (hardcover): 9781662949043
ISBN (paperback): 9781662939761
eISBN: 9781662939778

To Neil, Madeline, and Lilly
Thank you for always supporting and encouraging me
to write this book. I love you so very powerfully!

To my dad for always inspiring self-belief
"You are what you are"

To Nello, Angie, and Ida
For being my biggest cheerleaders

In dedication to my amazing mum.
You will always be in my heart.

Contents

Preface

I think I knew from an early age that I wanted to be a leader. I always gained my passion from dreaming, thinking big, striving for something more significant and impactful than I could do alone, and helping others gain self-belief to be more than they thought they were capable of.

I was fascinated by the long road, by the ability to realize something that had not yet been discovered. I was a daydreamer, often living in my own made-up fantasy world of impossible realities. I was creative, gravitating to the arts mostly in my comfort zone of isolation, spending hours drawing and painting. My mum always describes me as a quiet child: "You would hardly know she was there."

That changed in the years to come as I turned toward my love for the performing arts. I often put on a show, and the quiet child was often the loud one the adults desperately wanted to "use her inside voice." It allowed me to be something more, to express myself in a more outwardly accepting way. A chance to pretend to be something I was not and have others believe it.

That last part was important to me because I always felt different and subject to ridicule. In school, I was often made fun of because I read the words wrong and somewhat choked myself while reading out loud, inserting a fake cough to give me time to focus on the word I was struggling to articulate. Even just the anticipation of being mocked or laughed at would be the alarm that woke me each morning. I hated school.

The fifteen-minute walk was agonizing. My anxiety would build and build, as I imagined all sorts of scenarios going wrong for me. Then the self-talk would start. I was desperate to find answers. Why was I always behind everyone else? How come they all picked it up before I did? Why was I so bad at tests even when I knew the answers? Why did I muck up every time I read anything? Why did my breath fail me in the moments I needed more power? Why did I want to cry every time the teacher chose me to answer a question?

Everyone else in my family was so accomplished, super smart, and confident. Why not me? And that's the question I needed to ask but from a different perspective. Why not me? If they could, so could I. I just needed to figure out how. I was done with the why questions; I now needed to focus on the how. And that's when the confident artist in me matured.

I explored how I could use the strengths from my artistic endeavors to make me better at other things. I also gave myself some time away from worrying about what I couldn't do and went all in on what I could do.

As I mentioned earlier, I found my confidence through the performing arts. I practiced my craft, practiced, and practiced, failed repeatedly, stumbled on lines, and caught myself off-balance more often than not, but I just got back up and kept working on getting better. I rehearsed and rehearsed; my bedroom mirror was my best friend. Adjusting facial expressions, rechoreographing the movements repeatedly.

In the arts, I felt an acceptance of failing before achieving. It was a necessary part of the process.

No one judged or criticized. Instead, I was given encouragement and praise. When I found a different way that was even more magnificent than before, it wasn't seen as wasted effort; it was rewarded with praise, and then when on stage, applause and standing ovations! Wow!

As I turned my attention back to my academic career, I realized from my performing arts experiences that all I needed to do was practice, memorize, and rehearse, and when I couldn't do that, go slow, and inject personality into what I was reading, as though I were putting on a show.

All these creative endeavors came about for one reason. A need to escape my reality. I didn't feel I belonged. I couldn't easily do what was expected of me at school in relation to the set norms and standards. I was not naturally good at core academics. I struggled with the basics of reading and mathematics.

There was no recognition of academic struggles in those days. You were deemed "thick," unnatural, weak, an "idiot." I feared being labeled that way and was in constant stress mode, quietly sinking into a sea of social rejection. I couldn't let that reality be known. That was not an option for me. I worked hard to hide it. I worked hard in the background and felt accomplished with avoiding an F grade (although I had plenty of them), but mostly I managed the Ds and Cs, earning As and Bs in the creative/practical subjects; art; dance; PE; woodwork; metalwork; design.

I am thankful that I didn't have parents that obsessed over my grades or even cared if I went to school or not. They did care that I tried hard and worked hard, and that's what they saw me doing. I was also fortunate to have elder siblings that would support me if needed and were always there for me. But honestly, I was too embarrassed to ask for help at that very young age.

Later in life, I learned that my struggles with reading and math were due to a learning disorder. I see things differently when trying to function at the pace of others. The letters get jumbled up; the numbers are out of order. I have endured my fair share of reading something out loud and completely getting it wrong, much to the amusement of classmates and others. It still happens from time to time when I forget to slow down or am forced to read at speed (you'll enjoy watching me try to sing along at karaoke when I don't know the words already—it's shockingly bad).

Today I laugh along during those moments or call them out for myself first. I no longer see them as failures, just part of who I am. And those parts are what influence the strengths that power me today (just don't give me a timed test or any test, for that matter—I don't do well).

> **Out of my biggest fears have arisen my greatest superpowers and differentiate me as a leader today.**

I am known for being a visionary, a strategic thinker, and a compassionate and human-centered leader. I'm the one that sees the possibilities way ahead of others; I'm the one who unleashes purpose, passion, and greatness in others. All of that is fostered by the child who had to go slow and pay attention to detail to grasp the learning, comprehend, and understand. As a result, I can't easily multitask, so I am fully present for anything I show up for, fully engaged, listening with every sense, and getting overly excited by the curiosity to *really* understand. I like to ask questions, confirm my understanding, and validate my understanding, which causes me to need information from a variety of sources.

I'm curious to know why we believe something to be true; what are the other possibilities; what would be the ideal state regardless of what's possible. I also know that I don't have the skills to do everything that is needed to make a future vision happen and sometimes none, but I know I can find the people that have those superpowers, and I'm excited to be their biggest cheerleader in driving toward success.

I know that if I practice and I rehearse enough, I can tell the story that needs to be told to inspire others to take my daydreams and their own and make them a reality. I know that failing is part of the journey toward a better tomorrow. I know that from fear and discomfort, we embark on our most exciting journey, and when you are willing to face and embrace your biggest fear, you can become and achieve beyond what you think you are capable of.

You can go from a kid who's terrible at math and struggles with basic English to being a director in one of the top financial services companies in the US, having your own executive and professional coaching company, and being a published author. Now, what are the odds of that ever happening? The hero leader can make that a commonplace reality when they use their energy wisely and with the appropriate force.

I share this story with you to highlight that we are the sum of everything we have been and now are and the choices we have made, the influences we have been impacted by, the culture in which we have experienced growth, developed beliefs, loyalty to, preferences for, disappointments of, skepticism toward, nurtured our values, and so on.

Although the sum of what we are, based on where we have been, does not define who we will be. Instead, it influences the next steps we might take to any myriad of destinations we may choose for ourselves. Your path is as unique as the sum of everything that has made you what you are today, and it's essential that you understand what that unique journey means to the choices you make next, as a human first and then as a leader.

In the chapters ahead, we will explore the forces at play in the makeup of incredible, out-of-this-world, beyond-belief leadership. There is no magic formula. This is not the book where I will lay out the x number of steps to being the leader everyone wants to work for. Sure, you can expect to find some foundational traits, characteristics, and "things" as a constant in all good leaders. These are what I describe as surface-level expectations.

What we will explore together in these pages is what lies beneath. I know some of you are now visualizing Harrison Ford or Michelle Pfeiffer and drawing on horror movie memories. Well, that's actually pretty relevant because the prospect of reaching deep within yourself, surfacing all kinds of vulnerabilities, and swimming deep within the depths of the inner you is scary.

That's why we tend not to go there. The past is the past. After all, what good can come of reliving what you can't change? If we want to use our energy wisely, isn't that a waste of energy? My answer? Sure, *if* you skim-read or stroll down memory lane, or *if* you simply turn the pages of the photo album/Facebook /Instagram posts (which, by the way, only capture the moments you want to remember anyway). But if you take the time to stop and really look, connect to the emotions of the moments, spend time reading between the lines, you will find a broader awareness, deeper appreciation, reframed perspective, clarity of your values, and purpose through a lens you had never before given yourself the permission to appreciate. With these revelations, you will be inspired to cast your sights wider and farther.

Introduction

Becoming the person and leader you were always destined to be but didn't know yet.

The energy gained by going way below the surface of your inner being has a much stronger force than the energy behind staying in the safe zone at surface level. And with that force, you get the momentum to create the biggest and most awe-inspiring waves. You'll do less of riding the waves of others and more of creating the swell of waves that others go out of their way to catch!

Before we launch into the first chapter, I want to give you some background on my research. Much of it is steeped in my twenty-plus years of direct leadership experience. I've enjoyed a wealth of opportunities that I've captured and savored to varying degrees of success. I've learned a ton along the way. It's been both enriching and painful. The learning never ends. I continue to uncover blind spots. I continue to realize I have biases that I was convinced I didn't have. So much of what I write is in direct relation to my own experiences and revelations.

The second factor that features in guiding my writing is elevating the magnificent representation of leadership through the characters I never get tired of watching in superhero movies and series. They are all so very different but incredible, each in their own right.

Director Fury's strategic, distant, empowering leadership in *The Avengers* has you both frustrated and inspired simultaneously.

The righteous, human-centered, boldly strategic but obsessively targeted leadership of Wonder Woman.

The creative, innovative, novel, super-smart, but arrogant, sarcastic, and risk-taking leadership of Tony Stark.

The commanding, well-structured, organized, results-focused, selfless, but rigid leadership of Captain America.

The powerful, mission-driven, but sometimes reckless leadership of Captain Marvel.

The common theme in all is that they are all as flawed as they are incredible. It's from their flaws that their superpowers arise in a way that is unique to them. You can try to replicate it, but you will fall short. The whole package, warts, and all, create the perfectly imperfect hero leader.

Equally, I am inspired by the heroes in Greek mythology. Greek mythological heroes are known for their exceptional qualities and characteristics that set them apart from ordinary mortals. These heroes were often born with divine or semi-divine ancestry, which gave them extraordinary strength, courage, and intelligence. They were revered for their bravery, wisdom, and selflessness, and their stories have been passed down through generations, inspiring countless people to strive for greatness.

One of the most notable qualities of Greek mythological heroes is their physical strength. These heroes were often depicted as muscular and powerful, capable of performing incredible feats of strength and endurance. They were skilled warriors, able to defeat even the most formidable opponents in battle. Their strength was often attributed to their divine ancestry, which gave them an advantage over ordinary mortals.

Another important characteristic of Greek mythological heroes is their courage. These heroes were not afraid to face danger and were willing to risk their lives to protect their loved ones and their people. They were often called upon to undertake dangerous quests and missions, and they always rose to the challenge, displaying unwavering bravery and determination.

Greek mythological heroes were also known for their intelligence and wisdom. They were often portrayed as wise counselors and advisors, able to offer sage advice and guidance to their fellow mortals. They were skilled in the arts of diplomacy and negotiation and could resolve conflicts and disputes with their words and swords.

Finally, Greek mythological heroes were renowned for their selflessness and devotion to their people. They were willing to sacrifice their own lives for the greater good and were always ready to put the needs of their community above their own personal desires. They were true leaders, inspiring their people to greatness and setting an example of courage, strength, and wisdom for generations to come.

In conclusion, Greek mythological heroes were extraordinary individuals with a unique combination of physical strength, courage, intelligence, and selflessness. Their stories continue to inspire and captivate us, reminding us of the power of human potential and the importance of striving for greatness in all aspects of our lives.

The third factor that has guided my writing is the interviews and research with a multitude of magnificent leaders I have had the privilege to have been inspired by either directly or indirectly throughout my career. Each a superhero in their own right. It has been my humble honor to have been able to gather their insights and bring them to you in this book.

The constant theme that runs through this book is the different forces of energy that generate the power that perfectly imperfect hero leaders possess. No one set formula can be applied that suddenly puts you in the same league as these halls-of-fame-worthy individuals. The perfectly imperfect hero leader is inside you! You just may not have found it yet, or maybe you have, you just haven't figured out how to elevate it, or you are afraid to unleash that power for fear of a myriad of very valid reasons, or you're deliberately holding it in, as you find one more thing after another before you're ready for the big reveal.

That last one is the most common trait I see in emerging incredible leaders—they are convinced they are not ready and begin to live the false thoughts they conjure to keep them squarely within their safe zone. It's an incredibly safe zone, don't get me wrong, but there's more to be given beyond the boundaries of their safe zones. They will have a very valid, fact-based set of reasons that prove they are not ready until that moment of that thought-provoking, powerful coaching question that brings them the epiphany of their self-depriving tendencies.

It's like a tidal wave of aha moments crash into them, and suddenly the door is now wide open to take that small step in the right direction. Wisely put by Jemma Simmons (Simmons, 2020) from Marvel's *Agents of S.H.I.E.L.D.*, "The steps you take don't have to be big. They just need to take you in the right direction." But that step only gets taken when the energy forces that we create and exist in are rightly situated to take us there and then to keep going, and then burst through the breaking point to a destination they never believed could ever be within their reach.

It's a constant journey that requires restful moments to refuel, charge up, and provide the strategically planned boost in key moments that matter. You need to know when to cruise, when to switch off the engine and cool down, when to have the engine running but sit in neutral, when to turn back, go sideways, slow down, or speed up. The perfectly imperfect hero leader is always in control or able to capture control. Do you know what's also always the case? They are never alone. They all have help to guide them, inspire them, counter their flaws, cheer them on, pick them up when they fall, provide the perspective they are missing, and provide them with the brutally honest truths they need to hear. In other words, energy can be self-generated, self-sabotaged, given, or taken. How you harness it, where and when, and for what reason is yours to orchestrate, rehearse, choreograph, and experiment with before you can truly thrive at being the perfectly imperfect hero leader. Want to learn how?

Then let's explore together on these pages. We will start with the basics and build on that from chapter to chapter. Remember, this book is not about outlining the x number of steps you should take to be an incredible leader. It's a series of powerful concepts that will take you on a journey of self-discovery. I expect everyone who reads this book to find their own unique answers. I want you to trust in the process and, more importantly, in yourself.

No one knows you more or better than yourself. Be honest with yourself, accept, and find beauty in your imperfections. Be willing to surface the scars and caress them with gentle appreciation; dig into the corners of the self-depriving habits you have formed, and truly seek to understand where they were born from, and from there, decide how you want to grow.

Keep the pictures on the mantelpiece. They are not to be forgotten. They have significance and relevance, bringing you power in many other ways. Leave space on the mantelpiece for the pictures you have yet to create. For true, perfectly imperfect hero leaders, those pictures will not be of you. They will be of those around you who have become perfectly imperfect hero leaders through your leadership. You're not creating followers of your success. You're creating the wall of fame of those perfectly imperfect hero leaders you would stand beside, behind, or in front of as they so require. These are your Avengers! Your Marvelous Leaders!

If you are still with me, I know you are all in on discovering the perfectly imperfect hero leader within. First, let me introduce the everyday superheroes that graciously contributed their insights, learnings, and stories to this book. These perfectly imperfect hero leaders are my very own inspiration!

This book is full of the collective insights provided and, in some places, you will hear direct quotes from my interviews. A massive thanks to so many, but in particular:

Nigel Morris, Co-Founder of Capital One and Managing Partner of QED Investors, is a highly respected and influential figure in the financial industry, known for his innovative thinking and entrepreneurial spirit.

Brandon Black, former CEO of ARS National Services, Encore Capital Group, and co-author of *Ego Free Leadership*, is a highly respected leader in the financial industry with a commitment to innovation and excellence.

Tracey Bannochie, retired COO of DCM Services, is a master of operational excellence, driving innovation that empowers and enables teams to differentially serve their customers.

Robert Lord, Chief Revenue Officer at ARS National Services, is an accomplished strategic business leader with a commitment to operational and business culture excellence.

Tim Bauer, retired CEO and now board member of DCM Services, is highly regarded as an authority in the recoveries management industry, driving high standards of compliance and partnership with industry regulators.

Kelly Paul, Senior Director, Client Services at TrueAccord, previously Head of Operations at ERC, is a leading figure in the Recoveries Management Industry, passionate about empowering and enabling top talent while leveraging technology and data to drive outstanding customer experience.

Blake Hogan, founder and CEO of American InfoSource, is dedicated to excellence, innovation, and community service. His leadership at AIS has had a significant impact on the public record industry and its use in the Financial Services market.

His contributions to the community have made a positive difference in the lives of many people.

Adam Cohen is co-chairman and CEO of Phillips & Cohen Associates, a global specialty recoveries company. Adam is a highly regarded industry figure leading the way in developing cutting-edge innovation that optimizes data analytics and compassionate customer service practices.

Energy = Power = Abundance = Thriving

Chapter One:
Power YOUR Leadership Impact!

O ne of my favorite coaching questions is "what gives you energy?" Without fail, this question always evokes passion, a deep sense of uniquely curated values and emotions, and a focus beyond the transactional nature of what makes a person function daily. It intrinsically conjures the imagination to create a sense of being that is greater than oneself. It is always wrapped in positivity and almost always involves collaborating, giving, helping, or lifting others.

I feel a surge of energy just in how others answer this question, and many seem to transcend to an imaginary place where at that moment, they can see a glimpse of the hero within! That energy is always there. That uniquely personal truth is always present, and it's powerful. Although often we can feel like it's buried and lost below the things that overshadow that power.

Scientists anchor to the belief that energy never dies. It's a constant continuum! As leaders, we often feel like our energy is a finite resource that can burn quickly. Our reserves can be rapidly drained. The demands of our environment, culture, and societal role promptly overtake us, and we find ourselves protecting the scarcity of that energy that is all-important to survive.

I admire the marvelous leaders who can harness the hero within more often than not. They seem to have an aura of unbreakable strength, either subtle or overt. They attract an abundance of what drives success for themselves and those around them. They seem to thrive when others in similar situations struggle. They can bring light, hope, and inspiration in times of darkness. They are the sunshine in the rain. People from all backgrounds and experiences gravitate toward them and feel compelled to drive and enable their vision. They don't wait for permission. They simply empower themselves to want to contribute to their cause. They, too, find the hero within and confidently strive to thrive alongside or in front of this hero leader. These are the leaders everyone wants to work for.

Is this just luck, part of their DNA, a result of knowing the right people, being in the right place at the right time, and superintelligence? My research has shown that some or all those things are true to a certain extent. But the most significant difference is how you choose to use your energy, where you place it, and work to amplify it deliberately.

This book will explore how to harness the energy to power your leadership impact, amplify the hero within, and thrive as the perfectly imperfect hero leader everyone wants to work for.

Mythological and Modern-Day Superheroes as Leaders

Marvel movie characters provide many examples of outstanding leadership and teamwork. The same is true for stories of ancient mythological heroes.

For me, these movies and mythological stories show good triumph over evil and address the same challenges we face daily as leaders. We can emotionally connect with them. So, before we explore what I have learned through my research of real-life hero leaders, let's turn our attention to what history and movies can teach us.

Let's take imposter syndrome as an example: The emerging leader must step up at a crucial moment with high stakes. It's overwhelming for them. They become consumed with doubt and fear of failure, and there is always a line in the script where they say, "Why me? I'm not ready. You have the wrong person. I can't do this." But what do they always have? The guardian/ sponsor/advocate/mentor/coach/family—name them what you will—they are the person or group of people that help them see their worth and give them the courage to take the next best step.

Insights—What Did You Learn?

- Even powerful heroes face doubt, fear, and shame.
- Every great hero leader has a faithful set of guides that amplify their power.

These guides help the evolving hero challenge the truth behind their doubt, lift them when they fall, and help them find their true power. And then the magic happens!

A Story of Bias Creating Dysfunction and Impeding Success:

The first *Avengers* movie brings superheroes together to save the world. As each superhero is introduced, they each form an opinion of their fellow teammates. The first half of the movie shows how bias erodes the power of this collection of superpowers. While bias exists, dysfunctional team dynamics prevail.

Tony Stark's (Ironman) similarity bias to Bruce Banner (Hulk) is overt and extreme. His ability to connect with Banner intellectually leads to a stronger connection. Stark favors Banner in contrast to his disdain for the rule-following Steve Rogers (Captain America). As a result, Stark deliberately excludes Rogers from important engagements and constantly belittles his contributions and ideas.

The biases formed are in part driven by limited information provided by Director Fury, which, together with distorted media coverage of each superhero, causes each to make assumptions about the other's worth. This lack of appreciation for diverse talent persists for most of the movie's first half. Each believes their way is the right and best way, unbending to compromise and blend strengths. Despite all being given a clear goal with consistent communication, the lack of focus in fostering a strong personal connection across this group leads to a lack of trust and overall dysfunction of the team.

Dysfunction impacts the results of their collective performance time and time again. They thrive at pointing fingers at each other and elevating their faults. There is no introspection on what they could have done differently to elevate and use their core strengths and superpowers. It seems hopeless. No one is guiding them to function more effectively as a team.

It takes a pivotal moment in the movie when an emotional situation hits everyone at their core. They now find a common connection to the previously defined goal. It takes on a whole different meaning, and there is a collective connection to a compelling shared vision of what success looks and feels like. They rise above their differences, embrace their imperfections, and recognize that their biggest gains would come from allowing each other's strengths to rise to the surface at the precise moments that matter.

Stark does a complete U-turn in his opinion of Rogers, and the same is true in return. They celebrate the reckless actions of Hulk when the time comes for his brute force strength to be unleashed to play his role in saving the day. What earlier in the movie seems like a lost cause, a mission that is impossible to succeed at is turned on its head as each perfectly imperfect hero leader comes to the surface almost organically to make the impossible possible.

Insights—What Did You Learn?

- Incredible talent alone does not breed success.
- Teamwork sits on the shoulders of trust and respect.
- Having a clear vision is good but useless if you cannot connect diverse talent to a common set of shared outcomes.
- A culture where bias is allowed to fester creates dysfunctional teams.

A Story of Perseverance:

In Greek mythology, the story of Hercules is one of great perseverance and resilience. Hercules was a semi-god born out of an extramarital affair between his father, Zeus, and a mortal. Zeus's wife, Hera, struck by jealousy, set about to destroy Hercules, but with each challenge, Hercules maximized his super physical strength and intuition to rise victorious. What sets Hercules apart from others is his tenacity to persevere against all odds, again and again and again. At each turn, he remains true to his strengths with humility and forgiveness. Never seeking revenge, applying judgment, or complaining.

Insights—What Did You Learn?

- Great leaders overcome challenges by maximizing their strengths and avoiding judgment and ego-driven actions.

- You can still succeed and thrive even when it seems like the odds are continually against you.
- Incredible leaders remain true to who they are and rise victorious despite what obstacles others place in their path.

A Story of Misused Power:

It's also important to call out that the hero doesn't always succeed; these are equally important lessons learned. Sometimes, our heroes can let power or ego cloud their judgment. There are many examples where the hero leader becomes blindly confident and, in some cases, arrogant, which in the short term seems to gain excellent results but ultimately leads to dysfunction and destruction. It's not a sustainable model for resilient growth and success. That fleeting moment of thriving through ego driven, selfish means quickly shifts its leader and all around them into survival mode. It's a hard place to recover from, and they seldom do.

There are multiple examples of good and not-so-good leaders overusing or misusing power, and while portrayed in its extreme in Marvel movies and superhero TV series, great lessons are learned. The dos and don'ts are demonstrated and wrapped in storytelling with which we can all connect.

Let's take the TV version of Oliver Queen (Green Arrow) as an example. An entitled son of billionaire parents, Moira and Robert Queen, who outwardly appear to be pillars of the community and run respectful businesses. Oliver has an air of arrogance and gains loyalty from misguided followers. His generous squandering of the family fortune with his elaborate parties and his disregard for others' feelings is amplified by doing things that feed a temporary need.

This focus on the superficial creates a thirst for constant repetition of the same meaningless social engagements. It gives him a false sense of worth to use to his advantage. Along the way, he disregards the true friendship of his best friend, Tommy Merlyn. He cheats on his long-standing girlfriend, Laurel Lance, with her sister Sara Lance. The arrogance of his betrayal leads Sara Lance to accompany him on a sailing trip that changes the course of their lives forever. Oliver is believed to have died along with his father, Sara, and everyone else on board. His survival on Starfish Island is a rude awakening. He quickly sees that his privileged upbringing has no bearing on the brutal reality of this island's history.

He needs to earn respect, work hard to develop new skills, understand the consequences of actions, how to create allies, form a few trusting relationships, and become selfless in the plight of serving the greater good. If not, he would die and cause the deaths of countless more. He found purpose in his darkest moments. That sense of purpose brought him back to Starling City.

But even then, his purpose lacked a connection to core values, ultimately resulting in him committing crimes to eliminate those on a list provided by his father. Once again, his path to successfully reaching his goal was misguided, fueled by an ego that made him feel invincible, justified in his actions, and in need of no assistance or support from his still-loyal friend Tommy Merlyn. He shut him out and used him as needed but failed to confide or trust in him. This ultimately made an enemy of Tommy later in the series.

He made mistake after mistake and became more and more distant from his family and close friends. He eventually found the power of love and compassion that set him back on the right path. He learned how to trust in others and grounded his actions in core values that helped him rise as a natural leader and defend his city and people with greater significance. It became less about him and more about the greater good, the everyday person that deserved to feel safe, heard, understood, and valued. His actions, driven by deeply connecting to his values and the community with care and compassion, led him to become Starling City's mayor in later seasons. What a turnaround, right? Like all heroes, he had a guide. Someone who was able to work with him to surface the goodness and quiet his darker side. Felicity Smoak.

Insights—What Did You Learn?

- When leaders are motivated by temporary superficial popularity gains, they inadvertently lose sight of what's most important.

- Ego clouds leadership judgment and corrodes loyalty and trust.
- Relinquish self-fulfilling control and begin to trust in others.
- Leadership gains power through community, connection, compassion, trust, and value-driven decision-making.
- Hero leaders create allies, form trusting relationships, and become selfless in the plight of serving the greater good.

Without exception, all primary characters in Marvel movies, superhero TV series, and mythological heroes have faced situations of which they are less proud. All have weaknesses that plague how others perceive them, and all have needed to be vulnerable to overcome their biggest obstacles. It's not a steady road. There are meaningful failures along the way that provide essential insights that will later elevate a key strength at the very moment it matters most.

It's important to note that weaknesses don't necessarily go away. In some cases, they don't even get resolved. Instead, with the help of trusted guides, the character/hero chooses to redirect their energy toward the strengths that make them great, naturally lessening the prevalence and impact of their weaknesses. By openly acknowledging what they are not good at, others are less concentrated on them, even willingly filling the gap for them, and have amplified appreciation of what really defines them—their strengths!

There are so many important topics that the Marvel movies/ series and Greek mythology bring to the surface, which I have given rise to in the examples above: diversity and inclusion; racism; discrimination; privilege and hierarchy; dysfunctional teams; teamwork; relationships; social unrest; social unity; work hard/play hard; work/life balance; mental health; fear-based leadership; empowerment; trust; inspiration; integrity; humility; courage over fear; bravery over doubt. I could go on and on. You get the point. But in all cases, greatness only happens once individuals and their leaders are willing to go beneath the surface at a human level to find their clarity, purpose, and value. The true, perfectly imperfect hero leader is born from this place of human-centered self-discovery. They discover what powers their greatness.

Chapter Two:
Tuning Into Your "Human-Force"

The COVID pandemic and social unrest have shifted the attention to the heightened need for human-first strategies in the workplace. The "human" strategy is intrinsic to the overall business strategy. Often, business goals and people goals are in practice at odds with each other. Not because there has not been thought to understand what talent is needed to do the work, but because the environment, culture, and systems are surface level. The work is being done by humans.

You need to understand, appreciate, and feed the human need first. If you want people to thrive at work, you need to manage the needs of the whole person first and at the core of your business strategy. Each leader needs to be given the latitude and environment to truly create a culture that embodies differences at varying levels across a multitude of dimensions. There are so many great companies that do a great job at building that culture. I've worked in one such company for over two decades.

Where I see companies, especially big corporations, fall short is where performance and talent management systems do not align with the values and culture at the core of what enables their strategic vision.

Where these polarities exist, you notice practices are built to align with the standard protocols of any given industry and common social norms for specific positions within organizations. You can argue that without them, we succeed by chance and let favoritism and bias dictate how we reward talent and drive talent growth. However, when these standards and systems start to define the ideal worker or industry benchmarks, and you calibrate to that, you inadvertently create an environment where conformity to the standard and functioning within the acceptable systems and guardrails creates a culture of mediocrity, inadvertently suppressing or delaying progress and advancement for many, including the company overall.

Growth and advancement still happen, but it tends to be for the brave few and often is accompanied by the privilege to spike in one accepted standard that allows them to forge a new path, rise through the ranks, and make amazing breakthroughs for the company. These moments are essential to making progress and should be celebrated.

Each one of these heroes that lead within prominent companies has worked hard to get there. But there are so many more of those heroes right within every organization's humanforce who are capable of the same if certain standards and systems were less of a talent and industry conformity machine.

The phrase "if it's not broken, don't fix it" comes to mind. If you assume that phrase is the system you are working with, when you see an opportunity to "make it better," you have a choice. Making it better will serve to bring an abundance of additional opportunities and significantly increase revenue. If it succeeds, this will benefit your career trajectory and secure you as a top performer. You also recognize that you will meet resistance because it means functioning outside of the system— the system that defines the standard of success. But if you take that chance and you fail, you then break what didn't need to be fixed. This could lead to a low performance rating and maybe cost you your job. As you deliberate the pros and cons, the majority of the humanforce will anchor to decisions that serve the basic human need to survive. So, they stay within the safety of the confines of the system and standards deemed acceptable more often than not.

Who succeeds in making the right impression is also wrapped in so many other variables that the risk is exponentially higher for those who are less like the majority of their co-workers. As a result, their communication preferences are less accepted; their credibility is often questioned; their opinion is often dismissed or ignored; their voice is rarely heard, and in their plight to be heard, are misunderstood as being disruptive, always interrupting, maybe even too aggressive in their approach. Often these individuals within the humanforce are inadvertently forced to play it safe. In reality, you and the company want to see your breakthrough and set a new standard to raise the bar, but only a few are willing to go there.

In my interview with Nigel Morris, Co-Founder of Capital One and Managing Partner of QED Investors, he highlights the importance of people and culture. He has so many great insights, I thought I would share the five most critical exactly as he represented in our time together (Morris, 2022):

1. **"Changing culture is hard. It becomes very quickly concrete, very brittle, and hard to change. Start as you mean to go on."**

2. **"Know who you are and what you stand for. Define your culture around that. That way, you attract people that are drawn to the culture."**

3. **"Having people with diverse views is critical in the culture of all growing organizations."**

4. **"Be really intentional about what you do as a leader."**

"I spend so much of my time working with young founders. I talk to them about being intentional about what you do as a leader and how you build the building blocks for culture, and how you execute that as you scale. People are smart and constantly looking for cognitive dissonance between attitude and behavior, between what you say and what you do. If you're saying one thing and doing another, the whole thing just is built on sand."

5. **"Mobilization of people and culture around the strategy is the magic."**

"Strategy is a thing that works at a point in time, and it may be brilliant, but the durability of performance comes from the ability to execute that strategy, and that comes down to culture.

You need to have a sense of where comparative advantage is, and then wrap the culture around it. If culture disconnects from the strategic, where strategic value can be created, you have a problem. But the mobilization of people and culture around the strategy is the magic."

Changing Tides

The tide is changing in a world of rapidly advancing technology, work/life shifts caused by the COVID pandemic, social unrest, and the war in Ukraine. The modern workforce is looking to find deeper purpose and satisfaction in the work they do. They are more willing to courageously say what needs to be said and break the traditions and stagnant thinking that hold them back.

It's not enough to bring back a paycheck and have an amazing benefits package (things that meet surface needs only). It shouldn't be enough; many realize they have options beyond their current employment. In a Josh Bersin podcast, a leading authority on global talent and trends, he found that when you compare the number of jobs across the US and then the number of people who have voluntarily left their current employer, over a third of working Americans are looking for new work opportunities.

During the COVID pandemic, employers all heard the tagline of "the great resignation" and experienced higher than normal voluntary attrition rates. Employee expectations are changing. The "hero" leaders out there recognize it means their workforce is wanting connection, to bring value, to fulfill an individual purpose, and to make a difference beyond the confines of the standard.

There needs to be trust, flexibility, and joy in the work they do! With all of these core needs met, the hero leader gets a business that thrives, with a workforce that is committed to the mission, to driving growth and continual success. And when you can create an environment where the workforce at the individual and collective level feel empowered, uniquely appreciated, and trusted to live their best lives, doing work they are passionate about and valued for, you also get loyalty, commitment, dedication, and passion that's sticky and infectious.

It's so much more than the paycheck and benefits if you want sustained growth and success. You don't just need leaders; you need perfectly imperfect "hero" leaders! You don't need a workforce, you need a "human force"! Again, it's back to the notion of energy. Energy is a force from which to take you to new heights of leadership success.

For the remainder of this book, I'll refer to what you know today as the "workforce" as a "human force." After all, the language we use makes a difference in how we think, feel, and act. If you want to be the leader everyone wants to work for, you need to think differently about what's behind how humans do the work you need them to do. What's the culture you need to drive your strategy, and are you attracting talent that can thrive both for themselves and within the culture you have created?

Insights—What Did You Learn?

- Human force vs. workforce
- Be intentional about the culture you want to drive your strategy. Start as you mean to go on.
- Be intentional about the diverse talent you bring into your organization and obsess about the data around people and culture for sustainable growth and success.
- It's not enough to create a Diverse, Inclusive, and Equitable culture if you fail to address the unconscious bias that fueled the legacy systems still in play.
- Making tweaks to legacy human force systems is not enough to make meaningful progress and lasting changes within a more holistically advanced thriving company.

Chapter Three:
What's Powering Your Quinjet?

The Quinjet is an aircraft that is powered by five engines. It was first introduced to us by Marvel in 1969, but I think many Marvel fans may be familiar with it from *Agents of S.H.I.E.L.D.* The five engines of the Quinjet require equal force to perform at peak optimization. The exterior of this craft is impressive.

From time to time, it will receive modifications to adapt to changing needs, advance its impact, or expand its reach of capabilities. The engines may get fueled differently over time, but at its core, those five engines possess the power to make impossible outcomes a reality.

So, what's behind the power force of each of these metaphorical engines? Your own power forces. There is an abundance of different forces of energy, but for the purpose of this book, I want to focus our attention on five specific forces of energy. These will translate into reaching from the outside-in of your own Quinjet energy forces. Remember, this journey of discovery to expose what lies beneath the surface is scary. I encourage you to be brutally honest with yourself and to reach as far down as you can remember.

It's in the depths of these discovery moments that we can start to find what fuels and what drains these energy forces. Figuring that out will allow you to bring balance to your Quinjet. It's in the balance that we fire up the power that is indescribably uniquely yours. The perfectly imperfect hero leader leaves you wondering about the mystery that makes them so great.

Your search for the secret ingredient of their X factor, the missing element to answer the "Je ne sais quoi." What is it? You are often fooled that you've found it. You even ask these incredible leaders what makes them so special, and quickly dismiss the answer because it's often somewhat underwhelming. You get answers like "humility," "honesty," or even "I don't have any special power—I'm just me." What is it? Let me save you some time. Are you ready for the answer? I can feel the anticipation building. I feel like I'm about to reveal the holy grail of all answers that countless expeditions have been on the search for. Explorers have found a multitude of answers, and you've read everyone's lists of the things that make an incredible leader, feeling cheated out of your life savings. It's still missing the mystery ingredient. Well, here it is.

There is no single "it," no magic potion, no missing ingredient. "It" is the sum of every part of you—past, present, and potential future. It's as unique as your DNA. You can't copy it. You can't recreate it. It just is, because you are, you have been, you have felt, you have experienced, you have chosen, you have declined, you have won, you have lost, you just have! It's not about finding "it," it's about finding "You"!

While on the surface we may see similarities and connect with others through shared experiences even in different upbringings, there is often a core component of hearing other's stories that we can relate to or aspire to. You know those conversations. The ones that become like a tennis match, picking up speed as you realize "OMG, I never realized we had so much in common," "It's like we were cut from the same cloth," "Finally, someone who gets me," "Our paths have been so similar it's uncanny."

From these conversations, we find the courage to aspire to maybe something they have or have achieved, because clearly if they can, so can you. You are after all pretty much the same person, right?

Just because we can relate to someone by hearing their story, the details and the unspoken text between the lines, and the unique emotions and senses that built memory did so in very different ways. The environment and setting are almost always different.

The influences around you and the motivations that led to specific outcomes are part of a multitude of variations that make a connection point just that. A point of connection that you can relate to at some level.

The dictionaries (Oxford Languages, 2023) describe the word "relate" as "make or show a connection between" or "feel sympathy with, identify with."

I became increasingly curious about the concept of relatability as a perceived connection we might strive to find similar success to others. I see this a lot in my coaching. Often, people mistake coaching for mentoring. They come to me for my expertise and are looking to be given the answers or to find the answer by knowing more about my story and what I might do in each situation. I've been there, right? I've come across the same situations and struggles, right? So, of course, I will have the exact answer and formula to provide, and voila, the magic ingredient is suddenly all too clear until it is not.

Having a mentor or a bunch of mentors is vital to anyone's growth and development. It's part of the learning journey, but know that sometimes the things you take away will work, and sometimes they don't because the "thing" was within your context among the many unique variables surrounding your specific situation vs. the specific situation of the mentor you learned from.

It's not an exact science. I like to think of the things we mostly take away from our mentors as examples, options, and suggestions. Tried and tested data points that will certainly influence your decisions but not necessarily be the answers.

With coaching, you learn to find *your* context, understand *your* specific variables, and are guided to find the solution that best works for you.

Again, sometimes they work and sometimes they don't, but I often find that is due to something that changed in the variables, or something that wasn't quite considered, or just by allowing your self-deprecating inner voice to talk you out of doing what you said you were going to do.

More often than not, though, I find those who honestly dig deep and embrace an inner understanding that they had previously suppressed or neglected make the most remarkable advancements in their personal growth and impact.

They come to each coaching session not only nailing what they intended to but equipped with new revelations that they picked up along the way. It's like they found a new inner technology to tune in to and notice more about themselves than ever before. They encounter opportunities that they otherwise would not have even sought out. In fact, they find such profound levels of clarity that they operate with newfound self-assurance and belief.

This newfound power creates vibrations and ripple effects through and beyond their immediate network, emitting signals that invite opportunity toward them. I've had a couple of recent clients in this situation, and in both cases, they achieved their three-year career goal within six months of commencing coaching with me. The path to get there was all their making. I was simply the guide that helped them get there sooner. Of course, the coaching problem immediately shifted for both of these clients from elation and accomplishment to "Oh, Lord, can I really do this? I'm not ready. That happened too quickly. I think there are more qualified people than me."

Okay, let me remind you of the story I shared earlier where in almost every Marvel movie, when the hero is emerging, and at the very point where the stakes are high and failure is not an option, they become all-consumed by doubt and fear.

Now more than ever, the guide to these heroes is there to help them find their courage and connect to their purpose, to find the very thing within themselves that they can relate to moving forward confidently.

So, to clarify, emulating and mimicking others only gets you so far, but be sure to tune in when you are trying to be someone else and not who you are meant to be. It can also hold you back from your true potential and impact the pace of your unique journey. Why? Because it's not unique, it's been done before. Because it's not uniquely your way, it also lacks a certain level of genuine, authentic placement.

Relatability as a Desire for Connection

In his January 8, 2019, *New York Times* article, (Larson, 2019) Jeremy D. Larson wrote:

> Why do we want to share what is relatable? The French critic and philosopher René Girard suggested that all desire is mimetic, that we like things simply because we observe other people—our friends . . . relatability is a desire for a connection to the world, to want what we see in others—especially if what we see in others is ourselves.

Let me repeat that last piece again because I think it's extremely important in the context of what it takes to rise as the perfectly imperfect hero leader. "Relatability is a desire for a connection to the world, to want what we see in others—especially if what we see in others is ourselves." This line fascinated me, as it deals with two things: the act of connection and the feeling of belonging.

To connect with something or somebody suggests a bond that is formed, an interdependency or relationship, or some appreciation for similarities.

Equally, in the context of this sentence, Larson's words speak to me as relatability to others being a desire for acceptance, and belonging and in some ways requires a need for conformity.

This made me think about my conversations with the many incredible leaders I have interviewed for this book and many speeches I have heard about how the road to their success as a leader at times felt lonely. Not in a sad way, but in recognition that they were forging a new path.

There is equal space for conformity where it makes sense, and then there is a space for something new and different. There is an appreciation for the need for conformity traits and how to foster those relationships in a meaningful way. These relationships are fostered with relatability and belonging. It creates trust and safety. This foundation is super important when embarking on an uncertain path. The paths you might forge that can disrupt the sense of belonging and acceptance when what you look to achieve is beyond comprehension for many. Now that place of trust and safety is strained.

Some will journey along the vision and build advocacy, while others will hang behind in their comfort zone and remain attached to where they relate best.

As such, the perfectly imperfect leaders' strategic network of trusted collaborators will evolve and shift over time. There is nothing wrong with the group they previously associated with. They just have different paths forward. These incredible leaders have the courage to step out and in front with their newfound vision, attracting and detracting different groups of people. They are okay with that.

So, my question is, do we find the hero within by relating with other perfectly imperfect heroes we aspire to be like, or is it in the introspection to find our own inward relatability from where the hero within is born?

This notion of relatability and deep connection with oneself is where the foundation of our energy force begins. To be at our best as a leader, we first need to explore the core energy forces that fuel our state of being. As I mentioned previously, many energy forces impact us daily.

There are thousands of studies from which to choose. My research into the forces that enable perfectly imperfect heroes (fictional or real) finds concentration in these five energy forces:

- Mental
- Physical
- Social
- Cultural
- Environmental

Consider these five power forces as your Quinjet. On the outside, people see something spectacular. They study how you maneuver obstacles, navigate your terrain, gracefully glide through inspiring and stressful situations; and you are strong. At times you will take hits, and the dents will show, but you recover fast. They see you adapt to your environment with modifications that grow your capabilities. They feel a strong presence, especially when you are at rest. They wonder at the mechanics of how you operate with such stealth, resilience, and determination.

Each observer will come to their own conclusions. They will choose a truth that is befitting from the angle and perspective of where they are sitting. They will interpret your impact, value, and worth based on what they see, how often they engage, and how they engage; but do they really know what's fueling your engines? Let's take each energy force (your engines) in turn.

———· ⚡ ·———

Chapter Four:
Mental Force

This chapter is all about mental agility, the power of our mind, and how we think both subconsciously and consciously, how our thoughts manifest and how we behave, feel, and act as a result.

The brain is a magnificent and complex organ. It partners with the spinal cord and forms our central nervous system. The brain is our command center. It's the control system, working like a super advanced computer with sophisticated Artificial Intelligence (AI) and Robotic Processing Automation (RPA) technology fully built into the body's ecosystem.

The brain regulates our temperature, feelings, emotions, and breathing. It processes our thoughts and data inputs, organizes, and compartmentalizes them, and purges and stores information and memories. It drives our movements, vision, and hearing, and then it takes all of this and figures out how to operate the thirty million data points your brain faces at any given moment.

This happens primarily because of learned behaviors over time, eventually becoming behaviors and characteristics that are your natural state. You operate with the automatic pilot switch on for most of these second-nature activities and forms of thinking.

As a child, the act of crawling and walking is a mammoth task. It's a pattern of trial and error. It's the discovery of the order of physical placement, the practice that builds strength and stability. It feels and looks awkward, uncomfortable, and sometimes painful. You endure bumps and bruises, but eventually, you can stand for long periods of time.

You can take steps with the aid of the edges of the sofa to hold on to. You take that all-important first step with no support. You may have succeeded at the second step had the "big" people around you not jumped and screamed at you.

For a minute, you're a little taken aback, not sure what to make of the abrupt interruption to your starring moment, and then you realize it was "your starring moment" that got the big people all excited, and now you're excited and laughing.

As much as you want to repeat the action of that standing and stepping forward, your senses are overwhelmed. You don't know how to organize yourself, you want to stand, but that excited feeling is consuming part of your energy. It feels funny to stand and much wobblier than before, so you laugh, and whoa, the laugh monopolizes all the energy, and you're back on your bum again.

Each day, you keep trying to recreate the moment, and it happens again, this time with you taking a few more steps and so on and so on. As an adult, we barely have to think about what it takes to stand up and walk. In fact, we don't really consciously think about it at all. Our subconscious RPA system takes over, lagging your conscious thoughts and actions by about seven seconds.

Even then, a high percentage of those actions fail to register your conscious thought. They have become a habit. Have you ever driven somewhere and scared yourself because you don't actually remember the journey? You just know you arrived safely.

That's your subconscious taking charge. This is also how biases are formed. We gravitate to the familiar and act without thinking in given situations through autopilot mode. The brain registers a piece of stimuli (visual, auditory, emotional, etc.) and instantaneously seeks to connect with past similar situations and will jump the mind or action to the conclusions most reached in similar situations.

As you journey through life, you have found yourself in situations where you associate certain emotions with danger.

A vivid memory for me was riding my bike in the neighborhood and being chased by a dog fascinated by the motion of my pedaling. This dog was intent on snapping at my heels to stop the pedaling motion. I remember the instant rush of adrenaline, almost feeling lightheaded, my heart racing, and panic and anxiety set in. I hardly remember what actually happened. I just remember what I felt and the overwhelming need to peddle faster to avoid getting bit.

Eventually, the dog gave up, but I still rode as hard as I could to get home and safely secure myself in my room. When I reached my room, I was exhausted, my breathing was labored, my cheeks were red, and I felt super hot, and then suddenly that changed to feeling cold, weak, and tired.

It was at that moment I was flooded with emotion. Despite now being in the safety of my room and having a sense of relief, I burst into uncontrollable tears. This was my first recollection of the true fight-or-flight instinct kicking in. It was powerful and necessary for me to avoid pain. That was another example for my conscious brain to take, store, and convert to my subconscious memory bank.

Interestingly, in its subconscious state, the brain does not distinguish between real danger and perceived danger. If the subconscious mind detects a rising heart rate and a burst of adrenaline, it will automatically connect its association to that sense of danger from being chased by the dog, and suddenly I am compelled to flee as my instinctive response.

If we don't take the time to tune in to these instinctive behaviors and analyze our cause-and-effect habits, we can cause ourselves to miss opportunities, insult someone without meaning to, make decisions that are counterproductive, and, unfortunately, negatively impact the ability of others to realize their potential.

These actions can, at times, be counter to our conscious intentions. We just don't know it's happening. It's important that we tune in to how our mind is working for us or against us and retrain it to optimize our mental power force.

In *Agents of S.H.I.E.L.D.*, agent Elena "Yo-Yo" Rodriguez was attacked by a bird-like creature called a Shrike. The trauma of the event that almost killed Yo-Yo rendered her powerless.

Initially, the team sought to investigate the disappearance of her powers through scientific investigation. They suspected the creature had poisoned Yo-Yo.

Agent Simmons worked to find an antidote but with no success. In the meantime, danger continued to find the team, and it would be down to Yo-Yo and her speedster powers that would be needed to save the day. With increasing pressure and anxiety forming, the team decided that maybe agent Daisy Johnson's diviner mother, Jiaying, might be able to help.

With the combined help of Jiaying and agent May, Yo-Yo connected the trauma of the Shrike attack with an early childhood memory of her uncle's murder. Yo-Yo recollects how she used her superspeed powers at ten years of age to save a necklace from being stolen. It had deep sentimental value to her, but tensions rose when the intruders saw the necklace was missing.

Ultimately, her actions caused her uncle's death. The trauma of her childhood memory was triggered by the trauma from the attack of the Shrike. Her subconscious resurfaces the earlier trauma and connects the two events through the similarity of the feelings.

As a result, her subconscious causes Yo-Yo's powers to be suppressed at the memory of how using her powers resulted in a negative outcome all those years ago. Digging deep into her memory bank gave her the clarity to explore overcoming that mental block.

Prompted by May's reassurance that she would "bounce back," Yo-Yo had an aha moment that helped her reframe her mindset and ultimately regain her powers, just in time to save the day.

What this storyline demonstrates is just how powerful our thoughts can be in influencing our feelings and ultimately impacting our actions. It touches on a few key concepts:

1) **The connection between deep subconscious thought and physical ability**. A forgotten/suppressed memory, often associated with deep trauma, can resurface years later when a similar traumatic event occurs. In those situations, our brains work to process that information

and send messages through the central nervous system that can literally render us physically unable to do things we would ordinarily have been able to achieve. While this is an extreme example, you can experience a similar correlation to how an emotion surfaced through some sort of trigger, which can affect your physical performance. Athletes who have suffered a setback or an injury that previously knocked them off course can do so again, even when they are at peak fitness.

This tends to happen when something triggers the memory, and then the emotion associated with that past event resurfaces. This leads me to the next concept.

2)   **Goals are hindered due to fear and doubt.** We saw in this example how outcomes can be severely impacted when we function from a position of fear and doubt, regardless of how much we may desire a successful outcome.

3)   **The power of conscious constructive thought**. Note I didn't say positive thinking. This demonstrates how author Carl Bene guides us to think about the difference between positive thinking vs. conscious constructive thought.

In this situation, Yo-Yo demonstrated a positive mindset, visualizing herself using her special powers to defeat the enemy and win the day. She is filled with optimism; she has used this skill to similar success multiple times before. She knows she can do it. Yet despite her constantly pushing herself and attempting to bounce back, she fails time and time again.

Now frustration sets in. Anxiety rises as time runs out, the fear of failure is real, and the feelings of self-doubt and disappointment mount.

Even then, she is not aware of the inner turmoil that is the cause but rather looks for external answers. It's not her; it's something else. She's been poisoned. Having ruled any external possibility out, Yo-Yo finally looks inward and is supported and guided by Jiaying and agent May, shifting her mindset to embrace her inner demons and consciously reframe her thinking to move forward more effectively toward her desired goal.

The goal didn't change. Positive thinking alone was not enough. Developing more conscious constructive thoughts was needed to blend positive visualization with a better, more targeted action plan.

4) **Asking for and accepting help is key**. Without the guidance, encouragement, and expertise of many, but particularly agents May and Jiaying, Yo-Yo would have remained stuck and taken longer to recover. Maybe

she would have given up at some point and never recovered, settling for less than she is capable of.

Scientists have long proclaimed a strong connection between mind and body. In other words, what we are thinking influences how we feel, and how we think and feel influences the way we act and how others act toward us. In his book *Breaking the Habit of Being Yourself*, Dr. Joe Dispenza (Dispenza, 2020) says, "How you're thinking and feeling have created your state of being and environment." Dr. Dispenza expertly fuses together science and spirituality with grounded studies in the field of neuroscience, quantum physics, biology, genetics, and brain chemistry to scientifically ground how, as human beings, we create a "quantum loop." This loop is a string of learned behaviors, built over time and within our environment, that wire us to function unconsciously in specific ways. His notion is that if we control the thoughts and feelings that have formed our unconscious characteristics and behaviors, we can break those habits and form new ones to create different outcomes.

Let's frame this in an example: When we are nervous or worried, our brain transmits messages to parts of our bodies in preparation to fight and protect. Chemicals are released, and we can feel nauseous and lightheaded. Our stomachs can ache, and we feel weak. These reactions and behaviors have been built over years of conditioning from personal experience and/or what we heard from our parents and others as we grew up: "Don't walk on that wall; you'll fall off and hurt yourself." Therefore, phrases like this stick with us and when we fall, our bodies now expect pain, and our mind starts to worry. Equally, when we are faced with a metaphorical wall to traverse to get to an exciting new destination, our mind is already conditioned to be on guard. We expect we might fall; we visualize the worst, and we work to protect ourselves from pain and embarrassment.

So, at that precise moment when we need strength, our mind wants to tap in to learned behavior of how to make the body react when the mind is flooded with worry. We also know that we can feed the mind with positive energy and thoughts in those moments. In other words, we can change our state of being from a position of weakness to one of strength. How many times have we had that moment when fear strikes us when we least want it to appear? Normally, when the stakes are high—a key moment in an interview for that dream job, as you are about to take the stage at a conference, as you are about to make that important presentation that will launch a lifelong ambition, or even walking into a doctor's office to open up and ask for help, finally.

When we choose to take back control, we do things like:
- Take a few deep breaths and quiet our mind.
- We relinquish the negative thoughts, "delete that program."
- Lift our posture and stand strong, ready to open up to what's ahead.
- Speak to ourselves with positive words: "I can," "I will," "I am," redirecting our energy to positive outcomes.

- Visualize the successful outcome. With your clear intention set, you move forward through that now wide-open, inviting door.

Before any of this can be effective, the perfectly imperfect hero leader is first grounded in who they are beneath the surface. They have allowed vulnerabilities to surface, in most cases invited and embraced the discomfort, and accepted their inevitable failure points as learning opportunities as a necessary means to create something great.

Our brain is one of the most powerful energy forces out of any others; it helps power each of the other four we will discuss in this book. There are hundreds if not thousands of studies of how visualization practice can manifest physical performance as if the practice had occurred physically. In Dr. Joe Dispenza's book *Breaking the Habit of Being Yourself*, he describes a study of musicians where half physically practice with their instruments. The other half practiced through mental visualization only and without the use of the actual instrument. Both practiced for the same duration of time, over the same number of weeks.

Regardless of the difference in approach, the studies conducted on the brain showed the same results. It did not differentiate or associate whether the memory was being developed through actual physical activity vs. mental visualization only.

When it was time to perform the piece live from both groups, there was almost no difference in the level of their performance to the audience. It's remarkable. To the subconscious mind, the performers had all they needed to play successfully because it had stored the memory of having played that piece with this instrument multiple times before; therefore, at the time of the live performance with the actual instrument in hand, the performer was able to play expertly from that memory store.

Later in the book, he tells the story of his own daughter's summer goals and how she used visualization to connect subconsciously to a reality she believed would come true despite her having no real means of making it happen. Guided by her father's practices in mental visualization to manifest actual occurrences, she continued to meditate and visualize the summer adventure she so desperately wanted to have. Over time, the visualization became so deeply ingrained in her subconscious that her choices and encounters brought the opportunity to her.

Suddenly, her visualization began to become an actual possibility. She found clarity in the plan that was necessary, and ultimately, her desire was no longer just thought but became real. It was one of her best summers and a real turning point for her belief in herself and what she was capable of if she truly believed it was possible.

The DoorS Methodology

I have long aligned with this concept and practice meditation and visualization every day. My study of the connection between the mind and performance was what inspired me to develop the DoorS methodology. I encourage the practice of this with my coaching clients and have a guided practice that anyone can use to practice the DoorS methodology through meditation. If you visit my website at www.doorseffect.com or sign up for the Rising Catalyst app, you will find access to the fifteen-minute guided meditation.

I created the DoorS methodology as a means to create a state of being that is influenced by a set of intentions we create in our minds. The way we think has a powerful impact on the choices we make, the paths we walk, the emotions we feel, and the opportunities we find or accept. I call these opportunities "our Doors."

I once thought that my fortunes and misfortunes were a result of fluke events that I had little control over. How often do we say things like "these things happen," "I was just in the wrong place at the wrong time," or, conversely, "the stars just aligned," and "I guess it was my lucky day." What if it wasn't a fluke at all? What if our state of mind at any given moment or over a collection of events produced a specific outcome because of the energy we emitted in that moment or over that period of time? As I began to chart past events, I saw correlations between times of uncertainty, low energy, and negative thoughts aligned with key moments I considered failures. Whereas in times when I felt invincible, powerful, and energized, I achieved my greatest successes.

Furthermore, I realized that three intentions I had set in my late twenties that I had no idea how to make happen have since materialized:

1. After ten years of struggle and nine fertility treatments, I was blessed with twin daughters, Lilly and Madeline.
2. A lifelong dream to one day make the United States my home came true in 2008.
3. My desire to rise to senior levels of leadership at work surpassed my expectations.

It wasn't that these personal successes didn't have their challenges, in fact, quite the opposite, but because the belief of success was so strong and the intention I had set was so deeply embedded in my subconscious mind, that my every unconscious decision caused me to gravitate to networks and opportunities that would direct me toward my set intentions. It was as though my intuition had elevated powers to attract the very thing I desired. My unshakable beliefs to achieve that which I had no idea of how to make true, just seemed to find themselves in my reach. Answers to difficult, sometimes impossible questions just appeared when I least expected it. I felt my environment and surroundings seemed to miraculously open up doors to take me closer to my desired intentions. It was almost as though some magical spirit hovering over me in the clouds was carrying those intentions above me all the time, gathering from its vast perspective to bring about a string of situations where "the stars just aligned." I guess it was my "lucky day."

The DoorS methodology is a sequence of five simple phases that we can use to shift our frame of mind either in the moment, in our daily/weekly routines, or with long-term aspirations. No matter what your intention is, whether requiring immediate impact or as a means to guide your state of being for the long term, this guided meditation program is a powerful tool to manifest sustainable success. Whatever that means to you.

Firstly, I know you're wondering why the letters for D and S are capitalized and the other three phases start with lowercase letters. There's a good reason for that. Let me outline each of the five phases of this methodology:

- D—Disconnect
- o—offload
- o–open
- r—redirect
- S—Set an Intention

While all five phases are important, your biggest gains will be through mastering the ability to Disconnect and Set an Intention. Without fully being able to disconnect, the following steps will be somewhat hindered by the distraction of other thoughts, tasks of the day, or issues of the moment, and so by the time you reach that moment of setting your intention, the message can become difficult to decipher among the noise that surrounds it. When you transmit that Set Intention out into the universe, you want that message to be crystal clear, with no room for error or open for interpretation. It's with that clarity that you operate with intention, and opportunity gravitates toward you.

This is not mindfulness, although some techniques of mindfulness complement this practice. Mindfulness is more about being in the present, while the DoorS methodology is more geared toward disconnecting from the present, transporting yourself to an alternate dimension through visualization, and creating the doors that will lead you to a new and exciting future reality.

Using guided meditation is just one approach and tool from which to practice the DoorS methodology. It takes time to feel comfortable and needs time and practice to get this right. You will refine this practice over time and when you get there, you will learn techniques to draw on set intentions you have created within moments and without the need to be in a full state of meditation.

Let's address the importance of the first phase of this methodology.

Phase One—Disconnect

Disconnect

We carry so much baggage with us each day, that it accumulates. There are the daily chores, the pull of social media, alerts demanding your attention from the all too present technology that sits in the palm of your hand, and workday routines that can be all-consuming and overwhelming.

Regardless of whether you are the leader of a large or small organization or the leader of your home, it can consume an exorbitant amount of energy.

If you were to visualize what this looks like, it would look something like the TV character *The Flash* running at full speed, visibly distorted in appearance, because they are moving so fast. So, to disrupt your autopilot and be effective at shifting your energy and mindset toward greater possibilities, you have to get out of the "speed force." If you just try to add something else to the already heavy load of your overwhelming days, it can only ever be but just marginally effective.

You're not giving it the attention or energy it deserves. Step, jump, or leap out of the "speed force," take off your Flash outfit and truly Disconnect. Stop, clear your mind, and be completely present with yourself. Focus on your breathing and rest. Just do that now. Stop reading. Put down the book for at least fifteen minutes and just sit. Close your mind, acknowledge, and dismiss interruptions, and just be for fifteen minutes.

Welcome back! Notice how you are feeling and how your attention shifts as you recommence reading.

In Heather Cherry's Forbes article (Cherry, 2021), "The Benefits of Resting and How to Unplug in a Busy World," she writes:

"The human body is built to thrive in a series of short sprints. This is why taking a break—even only for a few minutes—can offer you the refresh you need to persevere through your day. Breaks are brief cessations to work, physical exertion, or emotional stress. They promote mental health, boost creativity, increase productivity, promote well-being, reduce stress, improve mood, and strengthen relationships."

The science also tells us that stress creates chemical and hormonal imbalances and surges that if pervasive can lead to serious health issues. When we become stressed, cortisol levels increase, and our blood pressure and heart rate increase. Over time these can lead to heart issues and strokes, to name but a few.

It's essential that we build habits into our daily and weekly routines that help to regulate our emotions, to elevate positive and calming emotions, and minimize negative and high-stress-inducing feelings. Now, that doesn't mean you avoid stressful situations; it means you have the mental agility to face stressful situations with a sense of calm or positive excitement. We'll explore this further through a three-step tool I like to use in phase two of the DoorS methodology.

As well as the DoorS methodology guided meditation, I want to provide some examples of daily habits that are most effective to help you disconnect.

Disconnect Daily Habits:

1) **Three deep breaths**—this is the number one most effective way that everyone does and should use to bring calm and help you center and focus with clarity. When you are feeling overwhelmed, it can be easy to find yourself in a downward spiral, when you are about to walk on stage for an important address, when you're about to deliver bad news, when you're pitching for that all-important contract, when you are about to . . . (you fill the gap). The list is endless, but the common theme is that they all surface an anxious, nervous feeling. Your knees might go weak, or your mouth goes dry, your voice becomes strained, your stomach will lurch, you may be a little lightheaded, and, honestly, you may feel like crying. Take a pause and alternate your focus on three key objects for about thirty seconds while you take three deep breaths. On that last breath, center your focus in one place and now

you can move forward. Pick up where you left off and repeat as needed. Trust me, the dramatic pauses will make a positive impression and distract your audience from your previous nervous exploits.

2) **Cognitive balancing**—this is a variation on the first example above. This is useful when you realize you're running too fast and feeling disorganized; not sure where to start, you find yourself ineffectively multi-tasking, starting lots of things but finishing few in a satisfactory way, but you don't have a good option or the time to really step away. Instead, simply sit up straight and take your gaze toward the ceiling for five seconds, then take a moment to fix your gaze on an intriguing or calming object to your left, and take a moment to maybe smile and appreciate the object. Do the same but this time with an object to your right, and then to an object in front of you. Repeat these steps two more times, then check your posture to sit a little further upright, before rolling the shoulders back, ready to resume what you had been doing. You will find that your breathing naturally regulates and slows down as you focus on movement and concentrated gratitude for simple objects. As you return, you will now have the clarity of mind to start to organize and prioritize your thoughts and work.

3) **Five-minute drift**—no matter how busy your schedule is, make a habit to take a five-minute break from whatever you are doing, every sixty to ninety minutes. Take a bathroom break, go get a drink, step outside if

you can, and walk to another space and back (do not check your phone or email). Play some music, sing if the occasion allows, get up and do a few stretches, look at a painting, go look out of the window, and get Alexa to tell you jokes. This simple five-minute drift will serve to give you an abundance of energy to make it through the next sixty to ninety minutes more productively.

4) **Delete that program**—this is an in-the-moment tool to use when your values get triggered. Someone says or does something that has your emotions firing up inside. Sometimes it's just the presence of someone or something that for whatever reason, has you wishing you were somewhere else. I learned this tool many years ago from an amazing motivational speaker, whose seminars were my first introduction to the power of the mind. I attended Mindstore for Life and Mindstore for Business courses on multiple occasions. It truly did change my life. Thank you, Jack Black (not the actor), for bringing your amazing mindset insights and practices to thousands that have gone on to live fuller and more enriching lives as a result. To this day, I continue to use this technique to simply visualize hitting the delete key on my keyboard whenever frustrating emotions arise from in-the-moment triggers. In this modern day of constant Zoom meetings, it's even easier to use this technique. Whatever discussion is happening that has me vexed, I can easily nod my head, smile, and focus on the delete key and say to myself "delete that

program." It's just enough to get me through and past the situation.

5) **Mindful walking**—if you can find fifteen minutes in the morning and the afternoon, make it a priority to take a mindful walk, ideally outside, but if not, use what space you have inside. Clear your mind and focus on tuning in to your breath and the sounds around you; notice things around you, really focus in with gratitude, and deepen your observation skills to just see. Don't analyze or judge or bring any kind of examination into what you see. Just see and enjoy. You will no doubt be interrupted by thoughts of tasks or chores. The mounting to-do list will render you guilty for taking this time for yourself. Acknowledge it and smile it away as you bring your focus back to the present. You will feel refreshed and actually achieve at least 15 percent more than if you had not taken those two fifteen-minute mindfulness walks.

6) **Meditate**—meditation is a powerful way to increase resilience, and power up your resolve to take on any challenge. It's pure regenerative energy. From the quiet, you find the loudest roars of energy to power the strength of mind you never imagined possible. Yet I find that this is the hardest of all the disconnect tools for my clients to do. Often, it's the feeling of failure and striving for perfection in the practice that holds people back from finding the power of meditation. If not that, then it's the feeling of guilt in just sitting and clearing your mind. I promise you, we can all find at least fifteen

minutes or even an hour most days to meditate. You just need to choose to give yourself this simple gift. Use a meditation app to keep you accountable. I like to use the Calm App, and I start every day with just seven minutes of the "Daily Jay." Thank you, Jay Shetty, for jump-starting my day, which I often share across my network. This simple morning act and what I get from those seven minutes, inspires me to find additional time later in the day to fully meditate. Sometimes it's just fifteen minutes and others an hour. For me, this is by far my biggest energy booster and contributes the lion's share of my mental agility and resilience. It gives me natural cognitive balance.

7) **Stretch**—the final tool I want to share for practicing and building your ability to disconnect is by stretching. Whether it is at your desk, a deliberate ten-minute stretching routine each morning, or a yoga or Pilates practice, it works wonders for your mental strength as well as physical ease. When you can self-massage the tensions caught in parts of your body and release them through strengthening, you feel a freedom that sends positive messages to the brain that naturally quiet the noise. It naturally pulls on the rhythm of your breathing, bringing increased oxygen to the brain for increased strength and clarity. I also place getting a massage under this category, something I do at least once a month. It's a worthwhile investment for anyone, but particularly the perfectly imperfect hero leader.

There are plenty more disconnect habits that you may choose to build into your daily and weekly routines. These seven are the ones I find more effective and powerful in regenerative benefits to our energy forces.

Phase Two—Offload

Offload—now that we have taken the time to disconnect and build a solid foundation from which to regenerate our energy store, we next turn our attention to getting rid of the "things" that no longer serve us, weigh us down, hold us back, and tether us to a narrow existence.

To effectively offload what is no longer serving you, *I encourage you to use AAPP.* This is a system I have developed that is at the forefront of getting unstuck. It keeps you out of the "speed force" and gives you additional space, time, and energy to place elsewhere for heightened personal leverage. AAPP is what offloading is all about. So, what is it exactly? Well, AAPP stands for:

- Awareness
- Acknowledgement
- Prescribe
- Purge

In the TV show *The Flash,* I'd like to turn our attention to a character who constantly evaluates his life and discovers new paths that lead him from strength to strength. All the time, he is becoming aware of new perspectives and reevaluating his existence. He continually sheds his old skin and builds a new reality for himself.

I'm talking about Kid Flash (Wally West), the son of Detective Joe West. It's a very messy backstory, but I think it's essential for me to provide you with the context.

The backstory: Things between Joe and Francine West, Wally's parents, became toxic and dysfunctional. Francine's lifestyle and choices were causing dangerous situations for them and their little girl, Iris.

Joe made a difficult choice and removed Francine from their life, cutting off all rights for her to see her daughter, and they agreed to part ways and never see each other again. Iris grew up thinking her mother had died when she was little and had no real memory of her.

Unbeknownst to Joe or Iris, Francine had been pregnant with Wally when they went their separate ways. She did her best with very little and tried to work hard to adapt her dysfunctional lifestyle for Wally's sake. He was all she had left. Despite her efforts, she was weighed down by the many burdens she placed on herself. Every effort always seemed to fall short of the life she wanted to make for her son, and old habits were hard to put down.

They were often on the road. The long drives were a point of connection for Wally with his mother, but also inspired in Wally a love for cars and racing cars in particular. Street racing became a passion for him, and as his mother's health deteriorated, Wally would compete to fund the overwhelming and mounting medical bills.

It was exhausting, but the sheer desperation to bring in money to pay the bills made winning an addiction. He also enjoyed the adrenaline rush he got through racing. These two habits caused him to make bad choices. He found himself in the wrong circles and building relationships with unsavory characters. It got him into trouble, and each time the environment was no longer serving his thirst for the rush and the money, he moved on, eventually finding himself in Central City.

It is there that he encountered his father and sister, learning from his dying mother that he had an estranged family. There were so many examples of broken trust evaporating all at the same time. Emotions ran high. Francine was dying, and Wally had struggled to survive his whole life when there was a blood family that could have helped but didn't. Iris felt betrayed by her father for lying to her all these years about her mother being dead.

Even though she had a fantastic upbringing and an abundance of love from her father, she felt cheated out of a relationship with her mother. She felt abandoned by her mother—why would she not fight to see her and want to get to know her? It was all so messed up. To add salt to the wound, Wally learned of Joe's adopted son, Barry Allen (The Flash). It was as though Barry had stolen his father from him, given how well Barry had succeeded in life and the opportunities he was afforded. Wally couldn't help but feel jealous. It should have been him. He was his blood son, after all.

How AAPP applies: Despite all the efforts of Joe, Iris, and Barry to welcome Wally with open arms, he resolved to let anger, frustration, and jealousy guide his choices. All in all, he was hurting, and he needed time to rationalize his thinking. He had so much inner conflict that needed to be resolved before he could even consider anything else, even when the "something else" was love and support from an adoring family, desperate to make up for lost time and ready to right the wrongs of the past.

As the emotions begin to settle and he's allowed himself the permission to disconnect and sit with his feelings, Wally starts to become increasingly aware of the situation he finds himself in. He realizes he has different choices to make, and he needs to define and prescribe the remedies that will help him move forward. This realization helps him consider all angles, allowing him to listen constructively to others. He begins to appreciate the circumstances and perspectives of Joe, Iris, and Barry and what they could and could not control.

He reflects on their courage and bravery to put their fragmented emotions to rest in favor of helping this young man they barely knew but somehow had belief in, regardless of the trouble and mayhem he seemed to invite. It required intervention from his newfound family to show love and encouragement, deliver the harsh messages, stand by him through his mistakes, hold him accountable for his own choices, and help him see there is another and better way.

He spends weeks struggling with his inner turmoil but eventually lands on clarity of thought to prescribe the action plan to see him through to a better future with renewed purpose. It would be difficult, but he knew what he needed to leave behind, put down, and change for his self-prescribed plan to succeed. If you haven't watched *The Flash*, I would highly recommend it. While this is just one story of how Wally applies AAPP to reinvent himself for better and more constructive outcomes, it's merely the first of many examples. Each time, he lifts to even greater heights of importance and impact, constantly curious to find an even greater purpose than the last time.

I hope this story helped you connect to how AAPP can be effectively applied, but let's clarify the purpose of each step:

1. **Awareness**—tune in to emotions, feelings, habits, systems you work within, and processes you follow or resist.
2. **Acknowledge**—once you learn about yourself and embrace or accept what you discover, ask yourself how these serve you. Be honest, check in on your biases, and use an accountability partner, mentor, or group of friends to help you unpack it. What is really helping

you, and what is consuming you with minimal benefit? I would encourage you to employ a professional coach in business and life. They will guide you in a way that others will not. They are not there to be your friend; they are not there to give you the answers you want to hear. They are not there to give you any answer; they are there to help you find the correct answers for yourself, and they will elevate and bring awareness to you from deep listening, asking powerful questions, and holding you accountable. Throughout this step, you will better understand your conflicts, giving you the clarity of mind to take the next step.

3. **Prescribe**—with your newfound clarity in understanding your conflicts, you can now prescribe the actions you want to take. Where are you headed? What does it mean to you? What is standing in your way? What's holding you back? What do you need to change? Answer those questions.

4. **Purge**—now that you have answered the questions about your conflicts, you know your blockers. It's time to enact your prescribed plan by first discarding what is blocking your way. This can show up in many forms.

Examples of Blockers That Hold Us Back:

o   **Lack of Time**

This is the first reason I hear, but it's rarely the leading cause of what stands in their way. Generally, things run much deeper, and as a result, we create habits that justify avoidance of addressing the harder issue. Some habits we form in these "time-suck" scenarios bring temporary enjoyment but do not provide sustained happiness.

Example—checking social media and text messaging—this is rarely that productive and eventually becomes a chore, constantly checking to ensure you respond in a timely manner or don't miss out on the day's hot topic. You essentially become a slave to your phone. It is more draining than it is energizing.

> **Purge tip**—restrict your time on social media; set boundaries and limits; hold yourself accountable; turn off unimportant alerts; when focusing on a specific thing without interruption, put your phone on silent and face it down (take off and turn off your smartwatch). Cut back on what and how frequently you post, having assessed the return on your investments.

o **Negative Self-Talk**

This is another common blocker we all need to pay less attention to. Don't misinterpret this to mean ignore it. You need to absolutely hear and acknowledge the negative self-talk to get behind where it's coming from and shape it into something more constructive.

Remember in Phase One, Disconnect, when I spoke of building strategies that will help you face stressful situations with increased mental agility? One such way to do this is to reframe our thinking and language toward discomfort, failure, fear, and doubt.

This next tool I often use helps you acknowledge the emotion, name it, sit with it to frame it within a rational context, and then own the constructive measures necessary to move you forward. When helping coaching clients shift to thriving rather than surviving in stressful situations, I use the following three-step tool:

> **Purge tip**—*name it, frame it, own it.* Let's clarify the three steps in this tool to help build mental agility toward stressful situations and when negative self-talk tries to win you over:
>
> * Name the emotion—label it: doubt, distrust, conflict, fear of failing.
> * Frame the emotion—provide the context; rationalize truth from thought; frame a series of questions that will help you understand the emotion better. What's driving it? What's the worst that could happen? What's the best that

can happen? What's less likely? What's most likely?

- Own it—once you've clarified the situation, own the constructive action to move you through and forward.

o **Relationship Drains**

This is a big one. We all adapt and evolve in different ways and at different paces. This means that relationships that were once buoyant, enjoyable, rewarding, fun, engaging, meaningful, and loving can become stale, draining, and a burden you accept through the feeling of guilt and dysfunction. The more naturally caring and compassionate you are, the harder it is to step away from or bring increased distance to certain relationships. Depending on the nature of the relationship, your core values can work against you in taking the necessary steps.

Purge tip—look, I'm even struggling to be able to associate the word "purge" with this category. It's insensitive, and there is a deep personal connection conflict with this one.

In a work environment, there is somewhat of an unspoken expectation that if you move to another job, company, or department, of course, your relationship shifts, and this can be an easier transition for many. But close personal relationships are a very different story. I'll address the latter situation first.

With personal relationships—be honest with yourself and each other, talk it through, and agree to certain boundaries for the relationship from now on, identify where things remain stuck, and, where appropriate, seek professional help.

For shifts in professional relationships, set clear and honest expectations as you move from one set of relationships to another. Cut back on the time and frequency of those with whom you continue to want to remain connected but have less immediate benefit from spending your time.

The same can be true for those who provide little value yet continually draw on you, leaving you feeling frustrated, low in energy, and distrusted. If you must work closely with such an individual, face it head-on and tell them how they make you feel. Be fact-based in your observations and genuinely seek to find common ground. If things don't change, seek support from your organization's management or HR systems. If you find yourself stuck and lacking meaningful support and action from your leadership, then you have much bigger questions to ask yourself to define your next move.

o **Work Commitments/Expectations**

I haven't met an executive or business leader yet who doesn't feel overwhelmed with work commitments, and to even contemplate taking some downtime seems a ridiculous notion to them. When we run so fast, we can easily pile more and more on. In fact, we feel guilty when taking a well-deserved break, so we'll continue to check emails, fail to eat a proper lunch due to back-to-back meetings, and book work travel that conflicts with important family events, promising we'll make it up. Burnout is very real.

I have also never met an executive or professional leader who cannot make some changes to their working habits to find better balance and increase their resilience through tough and changing times. If you want to maximize your time and impact at work further, start by defining the key priorities and anchor to those as much as possible, and above all make it fun, engaging, and purposeful. Since our focus here is about offloading, here are some examples for you to consider:

> **Purge tip**—it matters how you start your days, so if you have early morning work commitments as standard, change that. Give yourself at least one hour for yourself every morning to balance your mind. Remove distractions:

- Make it a standard that early morning meetings from that time slot are to be avoided. Allow an ad hoc urgent meeting during that time if absolutely necessary.
- Avoid emails or phone use during this time— if you must, take fifteen minutes before to address anything urgent—set a "do not disturb" on emails and calls. Get the news highlights ahead of time or after.
- Avoid watching or listening to the news. You can get swept far too easily into emotion when watching or listening to the news, and like watching a TV series, watching the news can take more time than necessary—subscribe to get highlights you can read quickly to keep in tune with the news.
- Assess where you spend your time and stop giving time and energy toward activities that no longer serve you or are time-bound. If you have an administrative assistant, have them help you be accountable for attending and engaging where it best serves you and your teams. Here are some questions to ask yourself as you conduct this assessment:
- Is this for me to lead/do/attend, or can someone else?
- How urgent is this?

- What's most important for me to get to today, this week, this month?
- What's the worst that will happen if I don't do this today or at all? What's more important than this right now? Who else might be able to help or pick this up if necessary? Is it necessary?
- How is this process/management system/performance expectation serving me and my team/the organization?
- How could I be better using my time right now?
- Is there something else I'm avoiding that's causing me to spend more time than I need to at work? What is that and how do I address that?
- How successful am I at transitioning out of my workday? What do I need to change?
- Am I taking sufficient time during my workday for breaks? What routines do I want to establish to give myself mental breaks, savor my lunch, connect informally with the team and colleagues, and take care of my physical and mental being?
- What/Who is draining my energy each day? What do I need to do to constructively address that?

o **Social Commitments/Expectations**

Like with everything else, balance is needed to thrive, and that will mean different things to different people, but if you are at the point where your social life, habits, and engagements are taking over, you'll start to notice a few things.

Purge tip—You may find yourself:

- Wanting to say "no" but feeling guilty
- Feeling resentment that certain things always come down to you among your friends/family
- Having less time for other things you'd like to do or get to
- Feeling more tired than usual
- Getting more irritable at the simplest things each day
- Spreading yourself thin to please others but feeling personally unfulfilled

Ask yourself these questions to determine what you want to change and what you want to stop doing:

- What gives me the most joy? Am I spending the right amount of time doing that? What gets in the way of making the most of that?
- What are the simple pleasures that give me the most energy and take little time? Am I giving

myself the time to do those things? What am I filling my time with instead? What do I need to do less of or stop doing altogether?

- Am I overdoing some things in my social calendar? Why do I think that? What impact is it having on me and those around me? What should I do differently or stop?
- What are the ideal things I want to be doing in my spare time? How much spare time do I want to have? Why is that important?

Reflect on your answers, and be deliberate in rationalizing where you spend your time and what you do in your free time/socially that truly brings you joy and has a positive impact on those you deeply care for.

Remove the Blockers

This explorative process allows you to reflect on what you want and what's getting in the way. What I find is that much of what is standing in our way is completely within our control to change. You just need to choose to look at it that way and expand your thinking.

When you can do that, you start to realize that you have been letting others or circumstances drive your ship. Taking you to destinations that perpetuate a reality that when you really think about it, might not be the best choice you could have made. You shouldn't dwell on that realization, but you should certainly allow that realization to motivate a better path forward. One in which you are in charge of the controls and can steer your Quinjet in the direction of your choosing.

You will make wrong turns, you will learn things you had not planned for, and that's okay, so long as you are driving toward your best-self destination. Allow that to give you the courage to make necessary changes and offload the things, relationships, routines, practices, activities, and thought patterns that are no longer serving you and be willing to revisit this activity often.

Bad habits set in fast and easily, but good habits take deliberation and time to establish. Those bad habits will continually surface and knock you off balance. You must keep them at bay, which is hard to do on your own. As a coach, I see this all the time and I serve to remind my clients with awareness, so they can steer their ship back on course.

At this point in the DoorS methodology, you have now developed two energy-powering habits. First, with the foundational energy force that allows everything else ahead to have the greatest impact, by disconnecting. This has cleared your mind and provided you the space to think more clearly and deliberately. As you travel in your Quinjet, imagine that the clouds have cleared, and the air is pure. Even though the headwinds have dissipated through your ability to disconnect, making it easier for you to move forward, your Quinjet still has obstacles in its path to be cleared.

The second energy-powering phase of the DoorS methodology has also been established—offload. There's the mental offload: your ship is too heavy and carries too much weight. You need to lighten the load.

For me, this is often the negative self-talk, the doubts, and fears that I manifest when taking the brave steps forward. The replays of situations that didn't go as planned, that I'm trying to fix in my head. All it does is to further serve to remind me of the pain I felt and the negative outcome and does nothing to help me move forward constructively. I must let them go. Off the Quinjet they go.

I stand at a safe distance, at just the right altitude, to watch the cargo door open, and then I release the straps holding on to those mental strains and watch them go. I close the doors.

The Quinjet can move a little easier with less effort now. We still have work to do, though; there's a storm ahead and flying objects that are blocking your path; you may even come under attack from fighter planes from various angles. These are the outward-facing obstacles you now need to face and decide which you are going to blow out of the sky, which you are going to allow to provide you greater protection and support (your allies), which do you ask to move, and which can you maneuver around more easily with the help of your allies.

Once you have offloaded and cleared the path ahead, now it's time to think deeply about what course you want to chart for the journey ahead. Let's move on to phase three of the DoorS methodology.

Phase Three—Open

Open—this is where you start to expand your mind and thinking to be open to new possibilities. You are free from the things that have weighed you down and now can turn your attention to supercharging your energy forces.

Here, I encourage you to turn to your past successes and to the people or events that are your biggest inspirations. This serves two purposes: the first is to allow you to celebrate your wins and savor the memories, connecting to the memories of the journey taken and the feelings, emotions, smells, tastes, and sounds you remember at the moment your achievement was realized.

You can relate to other times in your past when things seemed impossible or out of reach, but you have proved to yourself that if you believe you can, then you will have success. These are your own personal stories that have deep meaning to you. But we can run so fast that we forget to stop and remember. In my interview with Blake Hogan (President of American Infosource [AIS], he remembers how the simplicity of his very first job brought him great success, not just in that moment, but also in his future entrepreneurial endeavors. Blake recounted how he obtained a job placing inserts within a newspaper. He got paid on a per piece basis. His first night did not go well.

He was exhausted but did probably 10 percent of what the pros were doing. He made hardly any money.

Here's what he did (Hogan, 2022): "I started watching what the ones who knew what they were doing. I copied their process. I did more than they did within about three weeks. I increased my pay quite a bit. That became the basis of Hogan Information, which was that if you pay people on an hourly rate in what I call an unsupervised manner, everybody reverts to the low. If you pay people to where they can make more money by being more productive, then everybody makes more money and the cost per unit goes down."

Blake's business model married a win-win for all. His belief was that if the people working for him valued and had pride in producing high volumes at high quality, they should be paid for that dedication and passion. In the age of data gathering that was highly reliant on data entry people, Blake did not concern himself with employee level and applying wage caps. He focused on employing the right people and compensated them according to productivity and quality. Most of his data entry employees were earning between $83,000 to $100,000 annually.

When Blake later sold Hogan Information, the new owners were astonished by the earning potential of these workers and quickly applied more traditional pay incentives for this type of work. The company's net profit margins were 58 percent when Blake sold it. That's before tax. It was off the charts, predominately due to the compensation model Blake employed.

The new owners were so focused on aligning to the going rate for this job type and level in the industry, they forgot to look at the right number. When profit margins began to tank, I wonder how much they remembered Blake's advice.

Well, here's his advice (Hogan, 2022): "Did you look at their cost per unit? Their cost per unit is the lowest cost per unit of any data we acquire. If you start worrying about how much people make versus what your cost is, you're going to impact your returns."

Blake continued to build many other companies and remains unshakably committed to working in ways others might frown upon. Blake is no stranger to being open to new possibilities and bucking the trend. He has succeeded at it time and time again.

A closed-off mindset and fear to buck the trend can stand in the way of great leadership success and the success of others.

Interestingly, Blake's backstory bucks the trend of taking learning from the past in many cases. In his upbringing, his remarkable parents gave Blake every opportunity to be and do whatever he wanted, not through privilege, but more to do with a forward-focused mindset, free of the influence to safeguard against what his parents' experiences may have been.

His family rarely spoke of their past heritage. It really didn't matter. Why talk about the past when you can't change it. Much better to focus on today and chart new paths for the future. Anything is possible when you function from this place, as you don't hold yourself to the failures of the past.

That lesson leads nicely into the second purpose for this third phase in the DoorS methodology: Harness the power of inspiration. Tune in to your past and center your focus on those figures that inspired you, and who you greatly respected. What is it about them that you cherish the memories of? What impact did they make on you? How did they encourage or influence the choices you made and the person you have become?

Consider that some of these influential figures emerged at a distance, maybe you didn't personally know them, or maybe they were simply characters in a movie or a historical figure. It doesn't matter. It just matters that you appreciate what you learned and gained from them, which provides you with positive constructive momentum to be at your best.

I call these people your inspiration council. You can call on them anytime through your thoughts and imagine what advice they may give you. What would they do? Or more importantly, how would they guide me to the right answer? Visualize the conversations that would unfold. What would you hear them say? How might they encourage you? What would you be feeling at that moment? What would your physical posture look like? What do you notice about your energy and confidence level toward the end of the conversation? What are you compelled to do differently? What do you now know to be true in what you can do?

You can pull on this visualization tool anytime and anywhere, but remember to build your strategic network of influencers, those you can trust and rely on to guide you in your life choices. A family member, a parent, a sibling, grandparent, aunt, or uncle plays an important role in shaping and influencing you.

In my leadership insights interview with Robert Lord, Chief Revenue Officer at ARS National Services, the memories and connection with his mother are powerfully strong. She came up repeatedly. He told a funny story of working in the same organization as his mother. She had this reputation of stark contrasts. People often told him, (Lord, 2022) "It's hard working for your mother; I would NEVER want to work for anyone else." He emulates a lot of what he saw from his mom and the impact she made. He says (Lord, 2022), "She pushed them, she drove them, she respected them, they felt protected, they felt valued, they felt pushed. She was a great motivator, encouraging people to work more than they typically would under other supervisors, but she really cared about their financial stability outside of the company. She knew how important their future was for them and their children and encouraged them to take advantage of every opportunity."

The story of Robert Lord's mom made me think of Wonder Woman. Inspired by her mother, Hippolyta, and her aunt Antiope. Both are very different in their influences and the character they build in her. The leadership strength, care, and compassion of her mother are where Diana develops a passion for being the savior of humanity, for bringing peace and joy through times of turmoil. She is driven to do good, protect the innocent, and fight evil, just like her mother as queen of the Amazonians was doing should man once again find their protected magical island. She would not allow them to disrupt the balance again.

She would lead the women of Paradise Island in a way that caused Diana to appreciate the order and structure necessary to keep her people safe; although as a child, she rebelled against the constraints of her protective mother. She was missing the context and experiences necessary to understand what the past really meant for their reality and the preservation of their future. Hippolyta tells a young Diana of how Paradise Island came to be and the horrors of the outside world that she desperately wanted to protect Diana and all other Amazonian women from.

Let's turn our attention to her second family influence, her aunt Antiope. A magnificent warrior and former general of the Amazons. She would secretly train Diana in combat. Diana had a keen passion to be stronger and braver than her aunt and worked hard to earn her respect and to one day beat her in their grueling training sessions. She learned to be courageous, face discomfort and fear. She would even find moments where reckless choices and bending the rules were necessary to rise to the heights needed to defeat evil, something she would not have gained from her mother's mentorship alone. This blend of two incredible women created Wonder Woman! Sounds remarkably like Robert Lord's mother. Don't you think?

Other strong influences can come from educators, mentors, and leaders within your chosen career industry. These tend to be people you know and have formed relationships with. In this group, you will find many guides to help you on your journey. They are the ones that will encourage you to take brave steps. They are your advocates, your cheerleaders, and promoters. At times they may be your competition, but you will find that they will root for you and support you regardless.

Why? These special guides in your life's journey inspire you to mastery of their craft. You gravitate toward them because you see something in them that you want. Even though your power is unique to you, what they have is compelling and fascinating to you. They recognize where you bring something uniquely different to the table. They can appreciate how you shine and thrive in ways that they, too, are inspired by.

This makes me think of a conversation with a client who was exploring other opportunities for advancement and was invited to apply for an incredibly enriching role. The first revelation is that she's advanced her leadership skills far beyond what she recognizes for herself. She is more than capable and has proved her value, with a solid reputation in the industry. Nevertheless, she is struggling to recognize that for herself. When she reaches out to a long-respected mentor, she learns that her mentor has already applied for this role.

My client considers her mentor much more accomplished than herself and begins to doubt her ability to do the role. Well, like all good mentors, despite competing for the same role, she encouraged her to apply, even carving out time to help her prepare, elevating her confidence, and increasing her self-belief. This motivated her to work through her doubt.

She is choosing courage over fear and bravery over doubt. She is building a deeper connection to her value and what she uniquely brings to the table and has the support of a trusted friend and mentor to journey with. She has more to gain than she does to lose, and with that, I see her energy rising, her confidence exploding, and a conviction to go after her true worth. Her true worth is so much more than she ever imagined before embarking on this exploration for the next stage of her career.

Oh, and by the way, within two days of reaching out to her network to explore other roles, she landed an incredible job offer from a trusted and well-respected figure in the industry, along with this second, even broader advancement opportunity. I think that data point alone says something about this incredible leader's value and worth. People are racing to bring her on board.

The other people you should invite to your inspiration council are those who inspire you from afar. These people can show up in so many ways. They may be someone of historical significance, or a current-day author, TV celebrity, movie star, community figure, or industry leader whom you don't have a direct connection with. Something about them compels you to strive for more, to be at your best. They fuel your curiosity or just simply make you feel a sense of pride, respect, and belonging through their presence or the words that land most relevantly with you. They spark the imagination, build your courage, and encourage forward momentum.

Now that you have supercharged your energy forces from your very own uniquely curated inspiration council, and tapped into your own past accomplishments and achievements, you are ready to step into phase four of the DoorS methodology.

Phase Four—Redirect

Redirect—phase four is all about figuring out where you want to redirect your energy and focus. Through phases one to three, you have created space and lightened the load by discarding the things that no longer serve you, and supercharged your energy by engaging your inspiration council and enhancing your awareness of your true worth in reflection of what you have already accomplished and achieved. Wow! Now your Quinjet is more powerful than it's ever been, and the sky is clear in all directions.

So, you know what you are capable of, you are inspired to achieve even more, and you have increased clarity toward your purpose and value. Now what? Where do you go from here? The opportunities are abundant.

For some, it may be abundantly clear where you step next. Honestly, you have likely known where you wanted to head for some time, even years, but have been so consumed by the things that have held you back, all you needed to do was answer your conflicts, put down what was not working, and now you are ready to move forward.

For others, it might not yet be that clear. You have some exploring to do before you land on the destination you want to journey toward.

Let's go back to some of the questions you started to explore as you discovered your social commitment energy drains and reframe and expand them a little further:

- What gives me the most joy? How can I amplify that?
- What are my superpowers? How well am I maximizing them?
- What am I known for?
- What do I want to be known for in the future? What will that mean to me?
- Where do I want to be in my career six months, twelve months, or three years from now?

90

- How can I best describe my most immediate aspiration in just one sentence?
- How aspirational are my goals? Am I playing too safe? How can I reach further?
- How can I best describe my goal for . . . (use this sentence and apply whatever timeframe you want to focus on, i.e., today, the next three months)?
- What is most important about achieving my goals? What does it give me that I don't have today? What would it mean not to achieve them?

Now that you've explored, what have you discovered? Synthesize it and clarify it with a simple description of where you want to go next. Where is your destination?

Write it down. How does it sound to you? Tune in to the emotions that it raises. Are you feeling motivated? Does it feel right? What's right about it? How does it leverage your core strengths and align with your values?

Adjust as necessary, and when you're as sure as you can be, revisit offload if you notice fear and doubt set in. This is only natural when you are imagining something new and different. Once you have addressed any lingering conflict, refocus your attention back on your goal. Plot your course on your Quinjet. Fire up the engines and let it take you in the direction you want to go.

You are on a journey to a new destination, and while the skies have been cleared, you need to know how best to get there. When redirecting toward a new goal/destination, you need to establish your plan.

1. How long is this journey going to take?
2. What knowledge and experience do you need to pick up along the way?
3. Who might be best suited to help you on your journey? What variations of help might you need? How can you best leverage your existing network? What new network do you need to create?
4. Where do you need to make some pit stops along the way? What are you going to need? How can you best refuel, and how often?
5. What strengths are you going to pull on when you get stuck or take a wrong turn?
6. How will you approach difficult situations or learn something new that you hadn't considered before you started?
7. Who can you turn to as your trusted guides?
8. How will you keep accountable? Who can help you?
9. If you encounter a storm, what will you do?
10. What do you hope to be true along the journey?
11. How will you celebrate when you reach your destination? Who will you invite?

There are so many possible planning tools you can use. I'm not going to prescribe a particular one here, but I do want you to ensure a few things are true for you to transition from phase four to phase five on the DoorS methodology.

Phase Five—Set an Intention

Set an intention—now that you have worked to clarify your purpose and your goal, the plan needs to serve the purpose of achieving your set intention. When you can do the following, you know you are ready to set that intention firmly in place:

1. You are clear on your destination, and you know when you want to achieve it by.
2. You can connect to the value and importance of achieving your goal/s.
3. You have a plan.
4. You are prepared to hit turbulence and change course if necessary (flex your timeline if needed).
5. You know what and who you need to succeed.
6. You know who you need as your constant guides, supporters, cheerleaders, and accountability partners along the way.
7. You believe you can and will achieve your goal/s.

Without intentional time and thought given to setting an intention, we can get lost, lose focus, and be easily distracted. As such, we get off course and then we feel frustrated because we know something isn't right and we don't know what. We feel like we are failing more than we should and get stuck in this loop. It's often a guide or leader or mentor that gets us back on track, but sometimes it's an event or situation that can connect you back so strongly to that set intention that clarity is almost instantaneous.

In the first in the series of the Avengers movies, Loki of Asgard wreaks havoc on earth. He opens a portal into a S.H.I.E.L.D base to steal a powerful object called the Tesseract. In the wrong hands, terror and destruction would prevail.

Director Fury brings together an unlikely teaming of superheroes with vastly different talents and expertise. Their mission is clear and simple, and individually they know their role, but the truth is that their combined, collaborative efforts would be needed to complete the mission.

They initially work separately and somewhat against each other, failing to make meaningful progress. They become distracted by each other's work, opinions, and thoughts, and lose clarity on the set intention for their mission. Time is running out, and lives are being lost, because they each launched into action with little consideration for each other's contribution or observation.

At one point, Loki is apprehended by Captain America and Iron Man. It starts with Captain America appearing on the scene as Loki is about to blast an old man from existence due to his failure to comply with his demands. Loki and Captain America fight, but halfway through, Iron Man bursts onto the scene, using the technology in his suit to quickly defeat Loki, who simply surrenders.

Full of ego, Iron Man uses this victory to mock Captain America's efforts and dismisses Captain America's suspicion toward Loki's motivations, given how easily they were able to capture him and transport him to their base—a magnificent fortress with an abundance of all the latest technology suspended in the clouds.

Of course, this is all part of Loki's plan, but these Avengers had no real plan, they were simply seizing opportunistic moments for instant wins. It's not until Agent Colson is killed through Loki's planned escape and attack that the team begins to align to a common goal. They work together to clarify the goal, fully connecting to what success means. They form a plan, define clear roles and responsibilities, and respect and amplify each other's strengths, which ultimately enables them to win the day.

Loki's alien army is blasted back through the time portal that they came from, and Loki is handed over to his brother Thor to be held accountable for his actions back on Asgard.

Until there was clarity and alignment, the goal or set intention had a low probability of success. Even then, there needed to be a deep belief that success was possible. A clear plan was needed, and the team was prepared to deal with whatever came their way using their collective strengths and by working together. They kept each other accountable and on task. Failures occurred but they recovered quickly, regrouped, and strategically moved forward under the leadership and command of Captain America.

This final phase to Set an Intention is so much more than just stating the goal and writing it down. There is mental investment needed to deeply connect with the value and motivation for success. You need to be all in on reaching your goal. When an intention you set becomes so crystal clear and you are self-motivated to accept any challenge you may face, you're halfway there.

The plan you develop and execute and the people that help you get there happen almost organically. Your subconscious is omitting all sorts of signals, attracting supporters, and allies without you even knowing it. In fact, we just put this down to fluke good fortune most of the time or happy coincidences.

Trust me, they are not happy coincidences or fluke encounters; the opportunities found you at just the right time because you set the stage for that to happen. Your unbreakable commitment to your intention is transmitted to all who encountered you. You made an impression, you planted a seed to inspire collaboration, and you influenced investment. You amplified your intention out to the universe in all sorts of ways, through both intention and subconscious energy.

That's what makes the difference in driving toward a successful outcome. It's cognitive agility that amplifies the force of all the previous phases that powered your Quinjet. Your destination is reached and now you get to savor the moment, allowing all the senses to fully function to capture and store your achievement.

Power Up to Do Less and Be More

Now that you are familiar with the five phases of the DoorS methodology and how you can practically apply each phase, remember the story I told earlier on how the visualization of the desired intention can manifest success in reality? Supercharge your achievements and advance the impact and speed to success by taking the time to meditate on it each day. My fifteen-minute guided meditation will help you build this habit, and if you can stick with it each day for just fifteen minutes, it will change your life! The DoorS methodology guided meditation can be found on my website at www.doorseffect.com or on the Rising Catalyst App (find it on Google or Apple).

If you are not yet convinced by the power of the mind, let's take a look at what science and research tell us. Earlier, I referenced the work of Dr. Joe Dispenza and his book *Breaking the Habit of Being Yourself*. I was fascinated by the science behind his research, and so I wanted to take a moment to summarize what he presents.

Dr. Joe explores the potential of each person through the quantum field. He explores this through electromagnetic potentials and how they relate to our past, present, and future. It shows how our past connects our future potential as that connection point passes through where we are right now. The choices we make now are based on the depth at which we connect to our past and use them to form a future aspiration. He says (Dispenza, 2020), "All potential experiences exist in the quantum fields, a sea of infinite possibilities."

He goes on to explore brain wave patterns showing the correlation to how we feel and act. He elevates the importance of how we can best regulate those wave patterns and rhythms to help us be at our best, often.

An "incoherent" pattern or rhythm leads to dysfunction and stress, and a survival mode instinct sets in.

"Coherent" wave patterns and rhythms produce outputs that are more productive; we feel increased energy and function through what many call a state of flow. It just feels right, with infinite possibilities overflowing. When your brain waves flow with coherence, you have a heightened sense of emotional joy and gratitude.

The more elevated our positive emotions, the more constructive/productive energy we produce. In physics terms, Dr. Joe claims we use more energy than matter to function when sitting with more negative emotions, like doubt, fear, lust, competition, and judgment. That is when we feel burnout with the heightened sense of being overwhelmed.

Honestly, while I'm fascinated by science, it's not a place where I have any level of reliable expertise, so I look to the experts to help me understand it better. Please give me some grace if I haven't quite grasped it right.

The first thing that struck me here was this notion of our emotional state producing brain waves that function more on either matter or energy. So I did a little more research to try to understand the difference between matter and energy. (There's *a lot* of data.) The simplest way I have found it explained is through the Ox Science website. Simply put, (Ox Science, 2023) "matter is the substance that has mass and occupies space, while energy is the capability to do work." So how does that relate to the research of Dr. Joe?

In Figure 5A found in the accompanying PDF of his audible book, Dr. Joe writes, (Dispenza, 2020) ". . . the survival emotions ground us to be more like matter and less like energy. Emotions like anger, hatred, suffering, shame, guilt, judgment, and lust make us feel more physical because they carry a frequency that is slower and more like that of physical objects. However, the more elevated emotions such as love, joy, and gratitude are higher in frequency. As a result, they are more energy-like and less physical/material."

Okay, so this stopped me in my tracks a little bit, because the whole notion of this emotional state when we are experiencing fear, anger, or doubt, makes me feel like my energy levels have just gone into overdrive, and I'm quite literally all over the place.

To think that what's happening inside is somewhat counter to that outward feeling has my head exploding. Let me repeat what Dr. Joe says (Dispenza, 2020), ". . . they carry a frequency that is slower and more like that of physical objects." OMG! No wonder we feel stuck in those moments; we literally are.

So now I take the simple definition I found on the difference between matter and energy and interpret that to mean our ability to think and do is weighed down by the mass occupying our outward reactions. We are all over the place and become stuck and overwhelmed because there is no space to think or do. *What???* Help me out if I'm getting this wrong, but that's where my head goes when pulling all this data together.

In the reverse, when we are in "flow" and functioning at our best, the outward pace feels slow, calm, and graceful. Yet inside energy levels are high, pulling on less matter and functioning on rapid vibrations of high-frequency brain waves. Energy!

So, my question is why do we mostly take our cues on how to act or what decisions to make from the emotions we experience on the surface? It's almost as though in times when that stimuli process stress, we should get into the habit of flipping it on its head (except when we are experiencing "real" danger).

This takes me back to the earlier story of agent YoYo, who found herself paralyzed in using her powers exactly at the moment she needed to. She wasted so much time, at surface level, focusing on "mass," trying to conjure the physical action, that she gave herself no time to surface the energy to think. Outwardly she was going as fast as she could, trying everything possible, yet inside her energy levels and frequencies were at an all-time low. She needed to slow down externally first to give rise to the mental energy to thrive and then act.

There is so much more in the scientific research that I can geek out on, but I will spare you the details of my findings there. Let's conclude that stress and negative emotion slow our brain wave function, limiting our actions. Much better to self-regulate and elevate our positive energy, which in turn will increase our brain wave energy to better serve us when we need it most. We are now in "flow."

When We Are in "Flow," We Have the Energy and Mental Power to Level Up!

In season eight, episode one of the TV show, *The Flash*, there are great examples of leadership with a common term pervasive throughout. It charts how Flash along with other key characters have "leveled up" (*The Flash*, 2022). This term is what I'm talking about, and when it's described it ties back to the notion we have been exploring of functioning in "flow."

He has learned how to maximize his powers, slowing down "matter" and increasing his energy to gain clarity. There is a scene where Flash faces a criminal unit called the Royal Flush. Their leader can read minds and communicate instructions to her team through telepathy.

As Flash thinks through his next move to bring these criminals to justice, the leader of the criminal unit reads his mind and with the knowledge of what actions he intends to make, she gives instructions to her team to get in front of any of Flash's possible moves. But here's the thing, Flash has leveled up his skills, he's trained himself to be less impulsive and quick to act, giving himself the space to think with more clarity.

Combining this new skill with his superpower of superspeed and applying that strength to his mind as well as his physical abilities, he finds the formula to defeat these criminals with confidence and ease.

As the attack begins, Flash remains rooted to his spot, holding a smile on his face, shifting his focus slowly to his first assailant, and what appears to be in slow motion, moves her position so her strike impacts a colleague instead of Flash. He does the same with one of the other assailants, and then cuffs them all with tech that suppresses their powers before they can even figure out what just happened. They are confused. How was that possible? Well, here's how he put it (*The Flash*, 2022): "You can read minds. I can think in superspeed."

I put so much emphasis on mental force because it's the central point from which all other forces can thrive. I want to share this quote from LeBron James in his opening remarks in "Train your Mind—Vol 1" (Calm App) – (LeBron, 2020):

> This is LeBron James, and today what's on my mind, is my mind. A lot about basketball and life, in general, is about being in the moment. I can recall one moment in particular when my mental focus made the difference.

> It was 2012 and it was game three of the NBA finals. I'm sitting on the bench during a time out and I'm taking a rest before heading back in the game. To prepare myself, I wasn't doing ice packs or quad stretches. I wasn't having a trainer do soft tissue work on my shoulders. At that critical moment, I sat for thirty seconds, and I meditated.

> People talk a lot about my physical fitness. They see the sixteen seasons in the NBA and now seventeen. They see how I'm still going strong, and they want to know how I'm doing it. They want to know about my crazy training regimen and my diet. They want to know how I optimize my body. What gets talked about less, is how I optimize my mind and it's just as important.

> That's what I was doing on that timeout in 2012. I was gathering my thoughts and checking my emotions so I could approach the moment with a clear mind. There's

physical fitness and there's mental fitness. Physical fitness means strength, agility, and endurance. It means things like ground speed and air time. But what does it mean to be mentally fit?

For starters, it means presence, no matter what I'm doing, my attention is locked. It means awareness to see my surroundings with clarity and I can calculate my options. It means calm and composure in those big moments when the pressure's on. It means resilience.

I face a setback and I show up fresh the next game, the next quarter, the next possession. It means I walk into a room or step on the court and I'm at ease. I'm prepared, relaxed, and ready. And this isn't just about basketball. It's about life.

In closing out this chapter, let's clarify and synthesize what we have covered in a few easy-to-digest bullets:

Insights–What Did You Learn?

- Your mental force is at the center of all five of the energy forces that power your leadership engine (your Quinjet).
- The brain is our command center. It's the control system, working like a super-advanced computer with sophisticated AI and RPA technology fully built into the ecosystem of the body.

- Our thoughts have a powerful influence on our feelings and ultimately impact our actions. Before acting, consider:
  - The connection between your deep subconscious thought and how it's affecting your outward capabilities.
  - How your goals may be hindered due to fear and doubt. Answer your conflicts.
  - Harness the power of conscious constructive thought.
  - Who can best help, and who you should be accepting help from?
- Leverage the practice of the five phases of the DoorS methodology, both through daily meditation and through developing a rhythm with your daily/weekly and longer-term habits to:

  - D—Disconnect: make mental space to optimize the energy needed to thrive.
  - o—offload: supercharge your mental energy by offloading what no longer serves you.
  - o—open: open your mind to broader possibilities by tapping into your inspirations and achievements.
  - r—redirect: redirect your thinking toward future possibilities and clarify your goals.
  - S—set an intention: Be clear about what you want to achieve, with a firm commitment and deep belief. Visualize achieving your goals every day.

- Brain wave patterns correlate to how we feel and act. We can create new habits that best regulate those wave patterns and rhythms to help us be at our best more often.

- An "incoherent" pattern or rhythm of our brain wave frequencies leads to dysfunction and stress, and a survival mode instinct sets in.

- "Coherent" wave patterns and rhythms produce outputs that are more productive; we feel increased energy and function through what many call a state of flow.

- When we function with "flow," we increase our capacity to "level up"!

- In times when outward stimuli produce stress or negative emotions, or you are simply feeling stuck/demotivated, get into the habit of using the DoorS methodology to move you from survival mode (functioning at low energy, high mass) to thriving (functioning with high energy, low mass).

Chapter Five:
Physical Force

Our physical force is more concerned with external factors and how it creates the energy needed to balance our well-being, which in turn has a direct impact on our mental force. It's an outside-in type of concept. Of all the perfectly imperfect leaders I interviewed, there was a common theme for where they find their ability to disconnect and balance their energy—exercise.

From simple daily walking and stretching to marathon running, and mountain biking every Friday afternoon, each leader I interviewed created a routine that gave priority and importance to some regular physical activity. Two words you should tune in to there: priority and routine.

Taking care of the body and ensuring peak fitness, however you choose to define what that needs to be for the work you do, is all about creating endurance, stamina, and strength to perform at your best every day. It's a practice necessary for your success as a leader. Without it you can get easily knocked off course, you can sink into a problem and be wrapped in its clutches, feeling overwhelmed by the demands of the day.

With physical strength, you train not just the body to be strong but also the mind. This gives you the combined energy from two forces, mental and physical, to rise above any occasion and thrive. The leaders I interviewed for this book are stubbornly committed to protecting their time for their physical fitness for this very reason. It's super important and therefore a priority. Making this priority part of a routine is like their accountability tool. Committing to a certain time, duration, or outcome each day or week allows this priority to be formed as a habit. When we can make physical force routines a habit, we amplify their benefits and our impact.

A Tale of the Ups and Downs of My Own Physical Force

About a year or two prior to the COVID pandemic, my own routines were completely ingrained. I felt like a champion. I would wake up ahead of the rest of the house, tend to the many animals, hydrate, meditate, and then begin my daily yoga practice. Throughout my working day, I would ensure a few things were true:

- At least two, 30-minute meetings would be walking meetings.
- I would prioritize fifteen minutes in the morning and another in the afternoon for mindful walking.
- Alternate between standing and sitting throughout the day.
- Take the stairs rather than the elevator.
- Take a walk after eating my lunch.

My aim was to walk at least 14,000 steps a day, but most of the time I was close to 20,000 steps in any one given day.

Upon returning home after work, I'd take the dogs for a walk and on the nights my children had sporting or theater activities, I'd go for a walk for some or all of the time depending on if there was an opportunity to observe my kids' class. If the activity was close to my gym, I'd go and workout with some cardio and weights, which was about twice a week, and then I'd go for a longer workout over the weekend. It was like clockwork.

I had been carrying too much weight for years, which only got worse after the birth of my twins. But when I started this routine, I lost 60 lbs. I felt the best I had for a long time. All in all, I was doing the following each day:

- Thirty minutes of yoga
- Walking 14k to 20k steps a day
- Climbing four flights of stairs at least ten times

Then working out at the gym at least three times a week.

During that time, I was excelling at so many things in both work and life. My efforts were recognized even more than ever, my time with family was much more enriching and fun, and my social life was great. My thinking was clearer, and my joy for life was at an all-time high. My confidence soared.

And then my routine got knocked off course when I moved to a new job. I stopped prioritizing my physical fitness routines and on occasion my mental force routines. I was partway through a leadership program when I moved jobs, and it was taking up a lot of my time. My new job had a more challenging travel schedule, and it felt like one fire drill after another needed addressing just as I joined.

In fact, the fire drills just layered on top of each other, and I hadn't yet scratched the surface of understanding the department and how the work was done. The team had gone through a ton of change and lacked a solid management system and clear vision and goals. They operated in reactive mode 100 percent of the time. That was part of what had attracted me to the role in the first place, but I wasn't anticipating the perfect storm all hitting at once.

One of my twin daughters was struggling with anxiety to the point that it became almost impossible to get her into school each morning. That threw my morning routine and work schedule into disarray every morning for about two years. My husband was also struggling because of a toxic work environment and that spilled into the home environment. He became more isolated and depressed, and was functioning in victim mode for extended periods of time. This put strain on our relationship and his relationship with the children.

I was drowning, barely able to hold everything together. I knew as a family we could get on the other side of this, but it was going to take time. And then the COVID pandemic erupted and turned everything upside down even further.

The routines I had clung on to despite all that was going on just disappeared overnight. I had to re-create new routines and had little energy or motivation left to want to figure it out. I was able to keep up with my walking for about the first year into the pandemic and was able to do my yoga on occasion, but, overall, I had lost my habits.

The weight started piling back on. My priority was my family, and I kept a steady pace at work. I was surviving, not thriving in all aspects of my life, family, work, and socially. It was time to make a change. Step out of the speedforce and regain my mental and psychical energy. Without the full force, my aircraft was running at half speed but felt like it was being pushed past its limits every day.

I was waiting for the moment that it would just break or stop, and it almost did. I was given a warning sign that was more than enough to wake me up and get centered back to my routines.

I remember vividly the morning it all happened. I was actually having quite a calm morning. I was feeling at peace with the challenges ahead of the day and was just getting up from my desk to take a break and make an espresso. I put water into the coffee machine and while the water heated, I returned to my desk to close off an email I was writing. Once finished I could enjoy an uninterrupted break.

As I was typing, I noticed I was finding it difficult to navigate the keyboard and as I looked up to see what I had written, it was just random letters. There was no coherence, and I then noticed my vision starting to blur, particularly in my right eye. It was a little disorienting. I rubbed my eyes, but it just got worse, so I decided to step away from my desk and go make the coffee.

As I stood, I could hardly balance myself. I felt weak, and my limbs became heavy. Trying to lift my left arm to balance myself as I tumbled to the left failed me. I felt a sharp, searing pain in my head as I found myself half on and half off the sofa.

Both of my parents have suffered from multiple strokes, and I wondered if I was heading in that same direction, so as soon as I was feeling able to stand, I went and took an aspirin (my mom's wise advice). I sat for a while, still feeling weak and exhausted. I called my neighbor, who was upstairs helping my kids with their schoolwork, and she immediately sprang into action. She settled the kids and tried not to worry them as she drove me to the hospital to get checked out.

My husband met us there, and my neighbor returned home to be with the kids. After multiple tests and my strength returning, I left the hospital later that evening diagnosed with having had a mini stroke. It was a warning sign that deeply frightened me. I took the next week off work to just chill and consider what I needed to change.

The neurologist I saw some weeks later diagnosed it as an ocular migraine. That at least made me feel better. He explained that it was likely caused by my years of working from a laptop and hours of restricted blood flow due to how I was holding my head when working. I got myself an ergonomic chair, a desk that raised and lowered, and a monitor, keyboard, and mouse. I felt the difference almost immediately.

While I had maintained a good set of mental force habits, this was my sign to get my physical force back into shape. I started to build certain routines back into my day, such as the walking meetings. I even bought a treadmill that I could slide under my desk, and for long meetings that were more presentation than collaboration, I would walk and listen.

My excursions to the gym are still a struggle for me, and I have some work to do to get the right routine, but I'm committed to getting there. In all honesty, this is the energy force I must be most deliberate about, but when I find my rhythm and can combine the five forces in the right balance, life feels rich with joy and happiness. Success and accomplishments seem to come easily, even though there is an abundance of effort expelled. The challenges, and frustrations, pale into insignificance.

From Failures Come Our Greatest Successes!

We all have our high and our low moments, and as much as we choose to beat ourselves up in those moments where we feel we are failing, it's actually from those moments that we can grow the strongest. I've learned to embrace these swings in strength and clarity as a necessary part of transformational growth. In a recent *Bank On It* podcast by John Siracusa, Founding Fintech, Episode 2—"From Capital One to QED Investors"— Nigel Morris, Co-Founder and Managing Partner at QED Investors and co-founder of Capital One, talks about how when building Capital One and QED Investors, the number one priority was to find the right talent and enable a culture in which to grow and learn. His next words are what caused me to pause. He said, (Morris. 2022) ". . . keeping them at that growth edge, where they think they might be just failing, because that's where they are going to get the most growth and opportunity." I kept stopping, rewinding, and relistening to that sentence.

In one sense it resonated with my strong belief that transformational growth comes from waves of change, and directly out of moments when you feel at your most vulnerable and incapable. But this sentence seemed to be saying something more and I couldn't quite put my finger on it. The more I read it back, it seemed to indicate a deliberate, talent management system and culture that fosters and embraces pushing the boundaries of personal growth, which in turn ensures the continued growth of the organization and being at the forefront of transformational change.

In the main, that is what I have personally experienced at Capital One. There is a high propensity for change, there is a deep connection to the company's strategy delivered to all associates directly by the CEO. It's not a cascade, it's a three-day long investment from the CEO himself. This used to be the role that Nigel Morris assumed prior to leaving Capital One in 2004, and now Rich Fairbank has continued to maintain this as a key priority in the culture of Capital One. Empowering all associates to understand where the company is heading, and chart their own creative endeavors to help the company take the journey to "where winning is."

So, what does this have to do with physical force? Everything. No matter what your cultural background, any athlete, dancer, or fitness endeavor requires you to push beyond your current limits to grow and become stronger and more skilled. It's an accepted truth, because we have all experienced it in some way, shape, or form throughout our life, from learning to walk and ride a bike, to learning to swim and learning a new sport.

The list of physical activities is vast and long and everyone's experiences will be different, but in all cases, improvement comes from continually practicing, failing, learning, progressing with perseverance, and setting new stretch goals. Increasing the length of time, level of resistance, height, intensity, distance, and level of complexity.

As we learn, we fail more often than we achieve, but we push forward to find those moments for celebration. And—

yes—we stop and celebrate. We take note of the newfound muscle memory of what it took to get there, we discuss it with others, get inspired to become consistently good, and we even teach and encourage others to get there. We might share best practices, learn a best practice that helps us get even better, and once it becomes second nature, we ask ourselves "what now," and a new goal forms.

The feeling of achievement is infectious and if we maintain that momentum, we know we can "level up" again, and again, and again. At each "level up" moment, you feel like you are on the cusp of failing at multiple points in the process. On the treadmill as you are building your endurance to run faster, longer, and add in the incline that makes it harder, you *will* hit that point where your lungs feel like they are about to explode, your legs want to give up, your resolve is being continually tested, and to begin with, you cave into that pressure, but eventually, you break through that "burn" and once on the other side, you are on form.

You find your flow. A new personal best has been achieved. You pushed past your breaking point, and your subconscious just registered achievement on the other side of discomfort. So next time you are faced with pain and disappointment, your subconscious is learning to see that as an obstacle to be overcome and work through rather than to resist it and stop.

There is one last example I want to share with you to demonstrate how important it can be to "level up" your physical force. The Green Arrow of the Justice League (Oliver Queen) is probably one of my favorite self-made superheroes. On the surface, he is probably the most unlikely candidate for superhero status.

He is a self-centered, privileged, and a morally unsound human. He has no supernatural abilities. He is a normal "nonpowered" human with an abnormal ability to continually show up as a "jerk." Yet his circumstances of being shipwrecked on an island inhabited by ruthless drug smugglers forced him to make some choices if he were to survive.

For Queen, he needed to "level up" his physical force just as much as his mental force. He learned to run on rough terrain, climb, and increase his overall body strength, endurance, and resilience to a harsh environment. He honed his archery skills to hunt and defend himself. He experienced excruciating pain, a multitude of setbacks, and numerous occasions where he wanted to give up, doubting his ability to stretch his strengths any further. Nevertheless, he found the motivation to move forward, and gained peak fitness way beyond the realm of possibility for any human.

Without the rigor and routines to maximize his physical force, Queen would not have been able to achieve all that he did. Commitment to prioritize physical force routines brings the strengths not just for what you know you will need them for, but, most importantly, in the moments you cannot imagine or prepare for. Whether you believe it or not, you are capable and ready to rise and thrive, no matter what storms you face.

All in all, amplifying your physical force can have a positive impact to building the same commitment to drive past pain, failure, and doubt that we experience with mental force. There is a multiplying benefit.

Fueling Your Physical Power!

I've spoken about physical force in terms of activity and exercise thus far, but it's much more than that. It's also about what we choose to put into our bodies that can either energize us or drain us. How are we helping or disabling our bodies to function most productively for us? If we eat too many of the wrong things we can slow our digestive system down, we can clog our arteries, and even do irreversible damage to certain organs in the body.

If the damage we are inflicting on our bodies through our daily routines and diets were clearly visible to us, we would likely be more committed and motivated to keep them in better shape. What we do see isn't necessarily an indication of our physical health; weight alone is but one indicator among many. There are many other clues, and your energy level is a big one.

I like to think of Physical Force in its aggregate as a means to make you SHINE!

- S   Sleep
- H   Hydrate
- I   Inspect
- N   Nourish
- E   Exercise

When we SHINE, we show up outwardly at our best. We radiate energy, we demonstrate peak performance, and engage with clarity and purpose. The word itself has positive connotations. Current definitions in the (*Cambridge English. 2023) Dictionary* range from "To send out or reflect light;" "To point a light in a particular direction;" "To make something bright;" "To be extremely good at an activity or skill, in an obvious way;" "To show great ability in an activity."

When we describe people that inspire us or make a positive impression on us, we will use phrases like:

- He/She/They just radiate confidence.
- I've never seen their work shine so brightly.
- He/She/They have the ability to make things so clear.
- He/She/They are so bright.
- That discussion was so illuminating.
- They really shine at . . .
- That discussion really shed light on how . . .
- I can see things more clearly now.

Cheesy as it may seem, the connection between the words we associate with something or someone that shines is our outward physical being at its best! So, let's use this acronym to help guide what's needed to optimize our physical presence and performance. None of this is new or rocket science, but it's amazing how we can neglect one or multiple of the equations that make up SHINE.

SLEEP

Let's start with the importance of sleep.

It's our body's natural way of recharging and powering up. We physically cannot function without sleep, and we function at our best when we have enough quality sleep. Too much sleep, just like anything else we might overindulge in, does not lead to peak performance. So, what is the right amount of quality sleep? There are two things to address here: the right amount, and quality.

According to experts in this field, the average healthy adult requires between seven and nine hours of sleep every night. Children require more—up to thirteen hours from preschool age, reducing as we reach adulthood. The Nov 3, 2023 Sleep Foundation article by Danielle Pacheco and Dr Abhinav Singh, states, (Pacheco, Singh. 2023) "Sleep is an essential function that allows your body and mind to recharge, leaving you refreshed and alert when you wake up. Healthy sleep also helps the body remain healthy and stave off diseases. Without enough sleep, the brain cannot function properly. This can impair your abilities to concentrate, think clearly, and process memories."

It stands to reason that we make sleep a priority and routine (there are those two important words again—priority and routine). When we do, we lay the foundation by which we can SHINE.

The pressures of modern society have increased expectations of what we should be able to fit into our days. In fact, I see those who inevitably head toward a meltdown brag about how little sleep they need to function. In fact, it's impossible for them to sleep more than four to six hours a night. But they don't see that their body has adjusted to high productivity and little rest. Their mind doesn't want to sleep. It has too much to process. Too much downtime will make them lose that momentum. So, the mind works to only give the littlest amount of sleep to maintain the momentum.

This pace and a continual cycle of activity with little rest in between is not sustainable and inhibits progress to your full potential, even if you consider yourself to be highly successful. What that generally means in this situation is that you are successful at one particular thing and much of what life has to offer overall is compromised. You can be at physical peak fitness until the body can't take it anymore. You don't see it coming. It just stops.

If you want well-rounded success and joy in your life, sleep is extremely important. If you are already in a habit of high productivity and little sleep, it's going to take some hard work to form a new habit to prioritize sleep and target productivity toward fewer important things.

Overall, you will achieve more of what brings you joy and find momentum in elevating those fewer but more impactful and important elements of your life.

Numerous studies have shown how a good night's sleep can impact our energy, focus, and concentration. Why make things harder on ourselves? Too often in modern society, we seem to treat sleep the same way as building physical strength. We test ourselves on how much we can do on the littlest of sleep, then celebrate this as a victory.

Well, this isn't the place where you do that. This is where you take the victory lap on savoring a good night's sleep and waking well rested and with energy. It's from this place we will do our best work and have our best days.

Bruce Banner (Hulk) is a workaholic, and his transformations into the Hulk are disruptive to his sleep patterns. These two things have a significant impact on Banner. He is unable to switch off his brain, constantly sparking the imagination to explore further theories. It's a boundless, constant cycle of discovery that keeps him completely absorbed. No doubt this impacts his eating and exercise habits.

Too many irregular patterns dissolve the structure needed for optimal function. Banner's lack of sleep and poor care for himself leads to lack of patience; he is easily frustrated, which sets him back in both his work and relationships. Banner's anger is easily triggered and, as a result, the Hulk is unleashed.

It's not until later Marvel Avengers movies that Banner finally finds control over his anger; the result of a more structured and calmer lifestyle. One where sleep is of increased priority.

Equally, limiting and eliminating the frequency of turning into the Hulk naturally leaves him more rested. When Banner turns into the Hulk, he is unaware of what he is doing with the energy he is expending. To him, he may as well be asleep, but he's not. He wakes up exhausted, normally in some random location. His energy is depleted and it's difficult for him to find the energy to go about his day. He is often late for things and comes across as disorganized and lacking focus.

My daughter Lilly suffered with terrible night terrors for years. It was heartbreaking. She would wake multiple times a night. Her eyes glazed over as she stared through me and my husband, and she screamed with intense fear. It was as though she were in a horror movie she couldn't escape. She would run as though trying to escape something and would not let us come near her. In her night terrors, we were strangers to be feared.

She would wake in the mornings exhausted but none the wiser of the night terrors she experienced. Happily getting on with her day, with dark circles under her eyes and the palest of skin. She became irritated easily and would fall asleep anytime we got in the car or sat to watch a movie.

The first year was the hardest. The night terrors were frequent and lasted over ten minutes each time, multiple times a night. Eventually, they became less frequent and lasted maybe a couple of minutes, with just one occurrence per night. She functioned in this way for roughly three-and-a-half years.

When the night terrors finally stopped, that's when Lilly began to become super anxious during the day. The child that once loved school so much that she described summer vacations as a punishment, was now too fearful to step into school and other new experiences. She still has broken sleep patterns, which affects her ability to fully face her anxieties some days, but it is improving through the help of medication, therapy, and routine.

When she sleeps well, Lilly is like a whole different person— super outgoing and confident. Figuring out what triggers her broken sleep patterns has been extremely important to help her function at her best more often. It's still a journey and we hit setbacks every so often, but in all she is beginning to thrive.

Sleep disorders that are untreated can lead to serious health issues. It's important to recognize patterns and triggers that may be disrupting your ability to have a good night's sleep and address it.

So, what can you do to break poor sleep habits and gain a healthy sleeping routine?

First, let's address the definition I have in mind of poor sleep habits. Sure, there will be times when this is unavoidable, depending on what your schedule requires, but they shouldn't be part of your regular sleep patterns:

1) Irregular bedtimes
2) Absorbing yourself into things that keep you addictively focused on an activity within two hours before bedtime.
3) Eating a heavy meal within two hours before bedtime.
4) Drinking alcohol or caffeinated drinks close to bedtime.
5) Watching TV or checking social media within thirty minutes of going to sleep.
6) Going to bed angry/disappointed/worried/with unfinished business.
7) Sleeping in different places and locations (sometimes on the sofa, sometimes on the La-Z-Boy™, sometimes in the guest room, hotel rooms, etc.)
8) Poor sleeping positions
9) Surrounded by too much stuff and things that obstruct movement or comfortable sleeping positions
10) Irregular temperature—too hot

I'm going to point you back to the DoorS methodology and those two important themes that keep coming up: priority and routine.

No matter the situation that has me stressed, or left with low energy, there is something at the core of it that I need to start prioritizing and creating a routine for. In this case, we are focused on making sleep a priority and finding routines that best help us wake up energized, happy, and focused.

The DoorS methodology works equally as well in the evening as it does in the morning and during your day.

Bear in mind the ten factors above that I mentioned that can get in the way of you having regular restful sleep. Begin to explore the following questions to find what will work best for you:

1) What can I do to disconnect and quiet my mind before bed each night?
2) What do I need to offload to give my mind the space needed to prioritize sleep?
3) What routines am I open to explore to promote a good night's sleep? How can I open up to recognizing my accomplishments on the other side of a good night's sleep. What am I grateful for today?
4) What routines should I redirect my energy toward? Where should I redirect my energy and thoughts to

help me feel at peace with where I am ending today? What do I want to be true for tomorrow?

5) What intentions can I set for establishing a healthy sleep routine? Visualize what it feels like to wake up well rested each day. What is this allowing you to accomplish? Set an intention for what you are looking forward to tomorrow.

Before we move on, I want to double down on the importance of gaining quality sleep. Let's hear a little bit more about this from the experts. Dr. Michael Breus in his May 18, 2022, *Sleep Doctor* article states (Breus. 2022):

> A good night's sleep isn't as simple as just getting the recommended 7–9 hours each night. In fact, it's important to pay attention to your sleep quality in conjunction with how many hours you sleep each night. So, if you're getting a full night's sleep and you're still waking up feeling groggy and out of sorts, then there's probably another issue contributing to your poor sleep quality.
>
> During sleep, we move through several stages of non-REM sleep, followed by a stage of REM sleep. This is when your body processes memories, and also when you dream. Your blood pressure and heart rate also increase during this stage. Generally, the more time you spend dreaming in REM sleep, the less time you spend in the most restful stages of your sleep. This

contributes to you feeling more tired and less refreshed overall.

Signs of Good Sleep Quality

On the other side of the coin, here are some indicators that you have a healthy, restful sleep pattern:

- You wake up feeling refreshed in the morning.
- You feel energized during the day.
- You're focused, clear-headed, and in a great mood.

Cultivating Healthy Sleep Habits

Here are some of my pointers for you to work toward and ingrain a healthy sleep pattern. This is an alternative approach to using the DoorS methodology described above but gets to the same thing. Use whichever approach works best for you.

Start with some exploration and research.

1. When you are at your best, are you functioning closer to seven or nine hours of sleep?
2. Test out when is optimal for you to go to bed on a consistent basis.
3. What are the routines in the hour before bedtime that help you get a better night's sleep?
4. What are the routines in the hour before bedtime that disrupt your ability to get to sleep or to have a full night's sleep?

5. What can you do to cut out the things that disrupt your ability to have a good night's sleep?

6. What new routines can you build that give you optimal sleep? Test and learn.

7. Notate how you feel each morning and adjust as you learn from new patterns and data points that can further improve your sleep.

8. Adapt as needed when circumstances require flexibility to your routine. Even so, strive for at least seven hours of sleep and make an exception just that—a rare exception. Give yourself some grace.

9. Make it a priority to get back to the routine as soon as you can if you find yourself off track.

Establish the routine that works best for you.

1. Solidify your routine.

2. Now, make it into a ritual—pay attention to your senses—tune in to what you see, feel, hear, and taste with each task in your routine.

3. Practice gratitude for what your routine, turned ritual, is giving you.

   a. Establish three things you are grateful for before bed each night and repeat them again in the morning. Here are some examples:

      i. I am grateful for a restful night's sleep.

      ii. I am grateful for the energy I will generate/ have created.

    iii.   I am grateful for what I will achieve tomorrow/today.

  b.   Establish a thankfulness practice each morning and affirm what this gives you:

    i.   I am thankful for the clarity and energy gained from a good night's sleep.

    1. Today I am capable of anything.

    2. Today will be a good day.

    3. Today I will give the gift of *love, care, and compassion* (replace the last part with whatever values speak to you the most).

HYDRATE

Let's move to step two on your journey to SHINE.

This is going to be short and sweet. We all know hydration is paramount to a healthy body and mind. Our bodies comprise a lot of water, between 55 and 60 percent. All major organs in our bodies contain over 70 percent water. These organs are vital to our survival. When we get dehydrated, it can cause us to feel ill, lightheaded, weak, and we may even pass out. Prolonged periods without water can be fatal. Water feeds our cells, helps regulate our temperature, helps transport and metabolize certain nutrients in our bodies, keeps our joints supple, and much more.

It's *super important*! Drink plenty of fluids each day. Women need to drink about 11 cups of water a day and men around 16 cups.

INSPECT

Step three of SHINE is often forgotten, so I want to stress the importance to this middle child. Neglecting to give this step the right attention can cause your biggest regrets and trouble.

Life is precious but also very vulnerable to life-threatening illnesses and diseases. Advancements in modern medicine are quite remarkable, and with early detection, we can fight off, control, or completely cure most of these illnesses and diseases. The key phrase here is "early detection."

I'll be transparent. I'm not the best at this, but I do have an amazing doctor who holds me accountable for making my annual health visits, and she keeps me on top of making sure I'm visiting various specialists for routine checks.

At a minimum, make your annual health checkup a priority and be honest with your doctor about things you have noticed, changes to your body that you have questions about, changes in your energy levels, and your ability to focus.

Request a thorough check through blood tests and vitals. Ask what you should look out for or get tested for at your age. Depending on your family's health history, you may be at higher risk for certain conditions, and it's important that you are transparent about that and ask about what you can do to maintain vigilance and create habits that help lessen that risk.

As we age, our bodies and mental fitness change, and like with most other things, we must acknowledge that and continually learn to adapt. Lord knows I had pretty poor dietary habits in my younger years, but I felt fine, so I continued for years with unhealthy choices. I started smoking at an early age and it took multiple attempts to stop, but I did. I would drink far too much alcohol daily throughout my twenties and thirties, with a rich social life both personally and through work events.

Looking back, I wish I had made many different choices, but the past has served to influence how I choose to inspect my habits and how they affect my body and mind. I've realized I have a lot of control over addressing, limiting, and getting in front of habits that drain my energy and impact my focus. Living in that mode even at the height of confidence caused me to lack resilience and calm in moments of stress.

Prior to my corporate career, I was a schoolteacher and loved the kids I taught and the school I taught in, but when I piled on three major life events all at once, I lost all control of my emotions and my energy levels plummeted.

I moved to a new school, got married, and moved into our first home in a matter of two months. My unhealthy habits became the source by which I strived to cope with the stress.

I smoked more, I drank more, I slept less. It only made things worse, and I found myself in deep depression.

I had always been in so much control and confident in my decisions, and I just couldn't understand why I just wanted to close myself off from the world. I would drive to work considering driving off the road and ending it all.

At home, I would get so low and then angry at myself that I'd attempt to harm myself. I felt ashamed of what I was feeling, what I had become. I was on long-term leave from work and my husband removed everything in the house that I might harm myself with. I had hit the bottom, and I didn't know how to rise.

I'd missed all the signs along the way because life was good. I was excited about my next moves, but I didn't stop to take care of myself along the way. I didn't stop to inspect the lifestyle I had built and what it was doing to my body and mind.

It was through my recovery from my depression that I made some changes, including a career pivot away from teaching and joining Capital One at their Nottingham office as a phone agent. It was the structure I needed to help me rationalize my habits, pick myself up, and move forward in a different way.

It was not all smooth sailing. I found myself back with my poor habits at certain points, and there was always a moment that would tune me back to paying attention to making changes again. For me, this often came in the form of massive swings of high confidence to breaking down in the moment, with an urge to just cry. It mostly happened outside of work, but there were a couple of occasions when it showed up when I least wanted it to.

It wasn't until my mid-thirties that I really took stock of real change, driven by the desire to have a family. That wasn't coming easy for us, with multiple failed fertility treatments. The smoking stopped for good, the drinking was reduced and within normal limits; I got back into a routine for physical fitness and went to the doctor more regularly to check on my vitals, speaking more openly about what was worrying me, asking questions that I had become more curious about.

I made it a higher priority to continually inspect my physical and mental health, seeing more and more specialists to ensure I was on top of early detection for conditions I was becoming at a higher risk of developing as I aged.

The research led me to truly get balanced, and I picked up my meditation practices and started working with a fertility acupuncturist. I swear that along with those other life habit changes and fully inspecting how my mind and body were functioning, was what led to success this time around. In May 2010, our fertility treatment finally succeeded, and we were blessed with twin daughters, Madeline and Lilly!

Despite what I've learned about the importance of frequently stopping and inspecting my situation and choices, I continue to allow myself to fall into less effective rhythms and habits. What's behind that? Distraction.

I'm a visionary, a creative soul; my attention can easily be swept up by the excitement of a new venture, bringing to life new possibilities. I can often find myself forgetting to stop, look, and listen to myself and ensure I'm maintaining balance and inspecting my habits, body, and mind.

I cannot say I'm consistent with maintaining these routines and I often must get myself back on track, and that's okay. The important thing is that I take notice and make the necessary changes. It takes constant effort and work. I have lots of good reasons to commit to doing that.

A tool that I like to use when needing to refocus my energy to inspect my habits is something I call the "Cycle of Reflection."

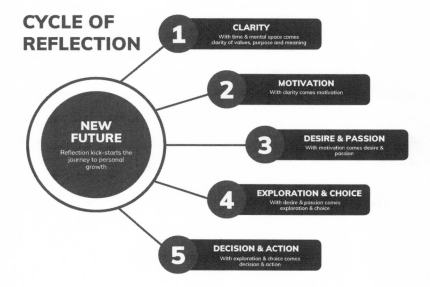

CYCLE OF REFLECTION

NEW FUTURE
Reflection kick-starts the journey to personal growth

1 CLARITY
With time & mental space comes clarity of values, purpose and meaning

2 MOTIVATION
With clarity comes motivation

3 DESIRE & PASSION
With motivation comes desire & passion

4 EXPLORATION & CHOICE
With desire & passion comes exploration & choice

5 DECISION & ACTION
With exploration & choice comes decision & action

We first must give ourselves permission to just be. Have space to think. Every day, we tend to leave these moments to chance. Something happens that sparks an internal conversation. Or if you are anything like me, you walk around your house talking out loud to yourself. It might also show up in a social engagement, sitting with a friend or a colleague discussing something that has caused you all to react.

Then there are circumstances that are a lot more abrupt and deliberate that prompt the "cycle of reflection" to kick-start. These are what I call the "shocks." These can be things like a new job, a restructure at work, a house purchase, a loss of a loved one, a loss of a job, or a health crisis. We can all relate to the shock the COVID pandemic caused. I'll use this as an example of when the "cycle of reflection" can show up.

Out of "Shock" Comes Reflection!

Gaining control over COVID levels and death rates, the world essentially shut down on many fronts to limit social interaction and left many without jobs or working remotely from the confines of their home. The knock-on impact from the shock of COVID created waves. Initially, people started to find new rhythms and norms to satisfy their basic survival needs. It's at this point when the aftermath of shock pauses to reflect.

Once we have taken care of the essentials to support our basic human needs, we naturally stop to reflect on ourselves.

How are we doing through all this? We explore our past and present with deep introspection.

This reflection allows us to unearth the values and purpose we have been neglecting in ourselves while stuck in the speed force of life. Usually, this self-reflection is short-lived. We get dragged back into what was and then continue as before. Procrastination sets in, and the feeling of something missing sits like sediment with us.

Only the very few stop long enough to notice new desires emerging. The isolation of the pandemic provided an abundance of time and mental space. Most of us took that gift of time and space to do our own reflection. We began to look at ourselves and life in different ways.

We leveled up our vantage point to see more and dug deeper into our true selves to connect to forgotten truths and desires. We found the "sediment." We'd written them off as the "dregs," but they are filled with unique goodness that needs to surface. Time to shake things up and start to taste the difference life can have. And from here, the great resignation was born.

But why do we wait for a shock to occur to stop and inspect? Truly remarkable leaders do not wait for those moments. They create those moments to not just inspect their business, organizations, and teams, and assess how they are doing, they do it for themselves, constantly.

I created the DoorS methodology I introduced earlier for that very reason. To create a routine/ritual by which to kick-start the cycle of reflection and determine the actions to arrive at a new future.

So, in closing this section, remember the importance to Inspect:

1. Your health—get your annual checkups, age, and family health history tests—early detection is key.
2. Your habits—how are you treating your body and mind to have resilience in moments of stress?
3. Your distractions—what do you allow to take you away from the most important goals you set for yourself? Answer the questions that need to be resolved that reduce the perpetual impact these distractions have on you.
4. Your deepest desires—don't let them sit like sediment waiting for someone else to find them. Lean in to aligning your choices to your purpose, values, and meaning.

A good coach can help you make meaningful traction on all of this, along with the regular practice of the DoorS methodology, either through meditation or practical application.

NOURISH

We are over halfway to shining at our brightest. We've touched on this fourth element in earlier sections, but I want to dial in on the different facets of nourishment. It simply comes down to what we are feeding our body, mind, and soul at any given time. There's a balance that needs to be achieved to function with flow, ease, and calm.

Okay, I know you are wondering where on earth did the "soul" part come from. Well, science calls it neuroscience and spiritualists may call it their faith. Here, I'm going to think of it as that inner being connected to a higher force or universal energy that guides what makes you who you are. The driving force behind what makes you happy or sad, capable or hindered.

It's not something you can see. It's not something you can really describe. It's a culmination of experiential imprints, either good or bad that we carry around with us, that our subconscious draws on with every action, decision, emotion, and feeling. It runs deep, so when past scars, pain, and trauma are prompted for recall, we emote in remembrance of that same feeling. We are rarely aware of the connection being made to those deep-rooted scars or moments of elation. We just know what we are feeling in the moment, based on the present situation we face, and we allow it to dictate our actions and choices.

When we do something that doesn't sit well with us, motivated by following a path someone else chose for us, we may use phrases like "I sold my soul," or "my soul feels empty," or "that's soul destroying," but when we conversely do something that has a higher level of satisfaction than one's own achievement, there's this uplifting feeling that's almost indescribable.

In these situations, you might use phrases like "It just feeds the soul," or describe someone you have a deep connection with as your "soul sister/brother." And when someone seems lost in finding their path or happiness, we might describe them as "soul searching."

So why is this important under the heading of nourishment? Whatever past traumas or celebrations we have experienced leaves an imprint. That imprint feeds the path we then are most likely to take. A pattern emerges. The question is what pattern do you want to be creating and which patterns do you want to redirect and improve on? Let's explore a little further an example of how those imprints get made. The starkest impressions are made from trauma and are the hardest to eradicate.

In *Avengers: Endgame*, we are introduced to a very different Thor. He is so used to thriving, forging forward despite all odds, and being humanity's savior. So, when he failed to kill Thanos in Wakanda, he placed all blame for what came next on his shoulders.

Many of his friends and half of all humanity are wiped out once Thanos gains possession of the fifth and final infinity stone. Thor becomes overwhelmed with guilt and regret. He replays what could have been over and over in hopes of a different ending.

The trauma and significant loss create an imprint of doubt and fear. The constant mental replay only serves to deepen the imprint. From here, Thor redirects his energy away from any situations which might result in the same failure. But here's the thing, his choices and decisions are now motivated by avoidance of failure, from which new imprints and patterns emerge.

One failure leads to another failure, and another, and another, and so on. The first time we see Thor in *Avengers: Endgame*, we see the consequence of these perpetual patterns of avoidance of failure and guilt. He's essentially a lost soul. He has isolated himself away from the world with two friends that are as equally self-absorbed and cut off from the outside world.

They spend their days playing video games and indulge in too much fast food and beer. He is grossly overweight and continues to sit with the heavy burden of his trauma, which shows up as anger. He finds laughter and shallow joy only in moments of complete intoxication.

Humorous as it may be in the moment, his temporary happiness is just a facade sitting on top of the burden he carries. There is no genuine joy or happiness; as such, it fails to create the imprint that can lead to happiness and success. It eventually takes persuasion from Banner and Rocket to entice him out of his destructive environment to begin the journey to restore his strength, purpose, and power, and eventually find his redeeming moment. Small steps in the right direction. Each win gives the confidence to try for the next win and the next.

From this example, we see the importance of what we feed the soul with. Feed it fear, anger, and disappointment and you will invite more fear, anger, and disappointment. Feed it with confidence, wins, accomplishments, gratefulness, and appreciation and you will invite more things to be thankful for and appreciative of. Success breeds success.

Rich Nourishment Comes from Surfacing the Truth

Thor's example also touches upon the two other elements of nourishment that need to be in balance with how we feed our "soul." Let's start with the mind. In this example, Thor chooses to place blame on himself. There is no substance to his conclusion. He was part of a team of equally motivated and skilled superheroes. There were multiple attempts to bring Thanos down. It was a team effort.

Thanos was aided by a guide who could see ahead to all possible events that might stand in the way of succeeding at his goals. He knew every move before it even happened, creating a big disadvantage to any efforts made by the Avengers. It wasn't Thor's burden to carry. These were impossible circumstances that the entire team could not stop.

Nevertheless, Thor created a dialogue for himself, feeding his mind with only negative speak. He continued to replay his failures rather than point his attention toward what he could do going forward to protect and serve the remainder of humanity. Feeding his mind only with the negative made him only see the worst of what else surrounded him. His mind now gravitated toward destructive thoughts, actions of anger, and a future of isolation, where he could do no further harm to the masses.

How we speak to ourselves needs to be constantly checked and validated. We often nourish our minds with made-up dialogue that we convince ourselves to be true. When that occurs, our actions are influenced by what we "think" to be the truth. It generally takes skillful questioning from a colleague, friend, mentor, or coach to help us see the lies we have been feeding ourselves. From there you can reframe the dialogue and move forward with informed and validated thinking.

And now to the final element of nourishment from this example. The element that you most likely expected this entire section of the book to be about. What we feed our body.

You heard in the Thor example how impactful eating and drinking the wrong things can have on our bodies. Sure, indulgence every now and then is also good for the soul. "Soul food" really is a thing, but too much, too often can have the very opposite effect in the long run.

For Thor, he gained a massive amount of weight and his energy levels dropped. He began to lose interest in productive and constructive activities, finding pleasure only in excessive eating, drinking, and playing video games.

Our diets help feed our bodies with the nutrients, vitamins, and energy we need to thrive. Even when we are dieting and trying to lose weight, it's important to eat a well-rounded, varied, and nutritious diet. Just eating less of the wrong things may meet the objective of losing weight, but it's not going to provide you the balanced nutrients and energy you need to thrive.

Spoiler alert—you are not going to learn anything you don't already know about eating a well-balanced diet. The average healthy adult should consume around 2,000 calories each day. Calories should come from five main sources:

- Fresh vegetables
- Fresh fruits
- Whole grains
- Lean proteins
- Nuts
- Legumes

The Department of Health and Human Services has tons of data and tools to help you define the right quantities of each of these healthy calorie sources. Remember to limit your intake of "empty" calories. Foods such as processed foods, cookies, fries, ice cream, chips, foods with high sugar content, and soda, to name but a few. I know. It's easier said than done. Notice that I didn't say avoid or eliminate.

I'm a strong believer that if you allow yourself a little of what's on the naughty list from time to time, we are happier and more likely to stick to a healthy balanced diet with greater consistency. Trust me, I'm speaking from experience. When I overindulge from the "naughty" list, I feel temporary satisfaction for sure, but my energy levels, motivation, and focus quite literally sucks. Oh, and I might develop strong feelings about the way I look, which depresses me even further into the family sized chip bag. Why do I buy the family size when I know I just bought the flavor only I like? It's clearly intended to be consumed only by me, not the family. Okay, seriously, as I'm writing, I'm salivating thinking about the dill pickle bag of chips that's calling my name from the pantry.

My brain is now trying to convince me it's okay to eat the bag of chips. I'm already overweight; this one bag of chips is not going to make a difference. I'll do better tomorrow. Umm, chances are I'll tell myself the same tomorrow. And when I want to go for a walk or do my exercises, I'll be too tired and tell myself it's my body's way of telling me I need to rest. So, I will rest and likely eat another bag of chips. And so it goes, the perpetual downward spiral begins.

So here I am again trying to find the inner strength to fight the urge to indulge off the "naughty" list. Maybe that's where I need to start. I am a self-confessed rule breaker, so present me with anything that is labeled naughty or forbidden, and my curiosity shoots through the roof.

If you're like me and managing a well-balanced diet doesn't come easy, what is it that drives you to crave more of the wrong stuff? What needs to be true to drive us to choose healthier options? This is a fascinating set of questions for me because my answers to the first question are not true. Let me share the list I came up with: "What drives me to crave more of the wrong stuff?"

- Convenience.
- Comfort.
- Tastier.
- Ease.
- It makes me feel good.

So, I asked myself, is it more convenient, comforting, tastier, or easier? Does it really make me feel good?

In each case, my answer was "no." Choosing fruit, veggies, or yogurt for a quick snack is just as easy and convenient. Actually, the foods I turn to for comfort cause me discomfort. They sit heavy and cause me heartburn. I prefer and gain more satisfaction from eating fresh vegetables and lean meats. I could live off asparagus, green beans, salads, chicken, or fish. They are my favorite foods. It takes me less time to prepare a healthy meal than an unhealthy one. And finally, while eating the unhealthy option feels great, I don't feel good afterward. I feel sluggish, tired, heavy, and in need of heartburn meds. As a result, I also find it harder to sleep, so I wake up a right old cranky pants.

Even just writing this has made me forget all about the nasty, greasy bag of chips I craved earlier. I'm now craving a nonfat Greek yogurt with berries. Excuse me for a moment while I indulge myself with nutritious nourishment.

Okay. I'm back. Let's explore the second question: What needs to be true to drive me to crave healthy choices?

In answering this question, I first needed to understand my motivation. For me, this is to have boundless energy, clarity of thought, and to feel light. My outward appearance should match that description. I have chosen to visualize what this would look like and pull on my past where this was true. I know I can achieve this because I already have; it's just a matter of taking myself there again. I remind myself what it felt like how my days went. It's inspiring and energizing to think about it. So, what were some of the habits I had formed, and how did I maintain them?

Shocker. Here come those two words again—I made planning my meals a priority. I developed a routine in the stores I would visit, the food I would choose, the meals I'd prepare, and the snacks I would reach for. I'd use the MyFitness Pal app to help me feel good about my choices, keep me balanced, and eat the right quantity of the right things. Seeing my achievements day in and day out was really encouraging and motivated me to keep going. I enjoyed celebrating my successes, and they were constant. Success breeds success.

So, what caused the relapse? I allowed changing circumstances to pull my attention away from these basic routines. The priority shifted toward a new job, a study schedule, and a constant flow of fire drills at work. Then COVID hit and messed up other routines, forcing this priority to the back of the line.

In truth, during these testing times, I needed boundless energy, clarity of thought, and to feel light. Instead, I deprived myself of the very thing I needed to replace it with short-lived survival measures. These measures soon became a habit until the day I realized I was feeling heavy, low energy, and everything seemed so much harder than it needed to be.

I also know that beating myself up for relapsing is not going to achieve anything. Instead, I choose to celebrate that I've recognized the mishap and am on the right path to succeed at reaching my healthy, balanced diet goals. The motivation is strong, and I remind myself of it daily through meditation and affirmations.

You've now heard my story and struggles with maintaining a healthy diet. It's constant work, which I'm grateful for. The challenge is one I have learned to embrace rather than avoid. A well-balanced diet is essential to fully SHINE, but it's not only about the food we eat. It's also about what our body needs to function at its best in all seasons of life.

As I have gotten older, my body requires different things than in my youth. My metabolism has slowed, hormonal changes have occurred, energy levels have become harder to maintain, and diet alone will not allow me to function at peak performance.

I have needed to feed my body with different supplements to help boost my energy levels. I'm at another stage of experimentation. What used to work no longer works; arthritis has set in, so I'm yet again seeking out the options available to me. I have been following traditional medical options for some years as my arthritis worsens and my joints continue to fail me. I feel like the Tin Man as I wake each morning. I want to be able to stand up straight with ease and place my feet on the floor without gaining shooting pains.

The only medication that seemed to have some benefit was methotrexate, but that wiped me out with each weekly dosage. While that lessened over time, I still felt more sluggish than usual and my mood was often low. I'd snap at my family for no reason. While the pain relief was great, the other side effects were not providing me the quality of life I wanted to maintain. There must be a better way.

I now have a variety of supplements I take that in combination are starting to help, but I know I'm missing something. Hence,

I call this phase a time of exploration. I want to caution that any decisions I make are well-informed by experts in their field. You should be guided by medical professionals in all these decisions and validate what you are hearing through your own research and through gaining alternative opinions and assessments. You are uniquely wired, and your needs will differ from others who seemingly are going through similar situations. There are too many variables to be considered upon deciding what your supplements and medication needs are. What's important is that you take the time to find trusted professionals and determine the options that will serve you best for where you are right now.

As you find the right formula, you will know. You will feel like a new person, renewed of energy. Enjoy being curious about what's working for you. Explore what it's giving you that you were previously lacking or struggling with. Celebrate the wins. Show appreciation and gratitude toward the gift you have found. Savor it. By doing this, you prolong the positive impact and benefits you are receiving.

But when you start to notice that something is changing in your focus and energy levels, don't forget to go back to the "inspect" phase of SHINE to begin the next adventure to explore what's next to get you back to peak performance. There's nothing necessarily wrong when what worked stops being as effective. It's just part of our growth and a signal that we are entering a new season in our lives. It's not wrong, it's just different. Our body just needs to be nourished in a different way.

In 2022 I started reading *LifeForce* by Tony Robbins, and I'm fascinated by the advancement in medical procedures that are less invasive and regenerative in approach. I cannot do credit to the abundance of great information in this book but would highly recommend leafing through its pages and geeking out on the stats, research, and findings. It, too, may inspire you to explore other medical options where relevant to you and your family. Again, while this book has significant contributions from medical professionals, you should always seek out professional advice and do your own research before making any decisions.

In fact, Tony shares a few of his own stories on what brought him to research and write this book. The result is a collaboration and business venture to bring the goodness found from the research to the masses. He was diagnosed with potentially life-threatening conditions that traditional medicine would require invasive, dangerous procedures, rendering Tony with the inability to do what he loves most in life and his career.

He sought out many alternative assessments, with a range of options, between nothing to highly invasive operations that had no guarantee of working but a high likelihood of impacting his energy levels for the long term. Neither spectrum felt right to Tony, and this is when he started to research further into regenerative medicines and stem cell procedures. He ultimately found the right solution for him, allowing him to continue to maintain his high energy levels and do the things he loves and thrives on.

EXERCISE

Now to the final ingredient to power your physical force in a way that makes you SHINE!

If you have done well at balancing all the other ingredients above, you have a solid foundation to thrive and grow stronger with your physical fitness. If you are running on empty, have neglected health concerns, or feed your body and mind the wrong things, it's just too hard to get a foothold in an effective exercise regimen. Sure, you can still exercise, but you will miss the full benefits if the other elements are out of balance.

There are varying degrees of physical fitness regimens that are generally dictated by your motivation. If you are highly competitive and have anchored toward specific sports or fitness activities, your exercise patterns and routine will be driven by the motivation to succeed and be at your best. If your motivation is to maintain a specific desired weight and look, the exercise choices you make will be inspired by that. If your motivation is to lose weight and gain muscle definition, your exercise activities will be inspired by that vision.

If you are to succeed at sustaining your physical fitness regimens, you need to first establish and be married to your motivation. Start with simple questions, and build from there:

1) How are you feeling about your physical activity levels?
2) How happy are you with the way you look and feel?

3) What do you want to be true?
4) What do you want to gain from reaching your goal? What will that mean to you?
5) What do you need to get started?
6) What will need to be true to sustain and maintain momentum toward your goals?
7) Who can help you keep accountable?
8) How will you know when you have arrived at achieving your initial goal?

Top tips: When you reach your initial goal, the hard work to sustain or improve on where you have arrived will become important. Make a point to celebrate your success; reflect on what was and what is now; show yourself gratitude for what you have gained; give thanks to the new you and then ask yourself, "What now?"

That last part is where I stumble time and time again. I've learned that I need someone to prompt me with that question and help me to continue to move forward. Without it, I continue to swing back and forth with my physical fitness, and it has ripple effects on all facets of physical energy.

When Barry Allen (The Flash), first gained his powers, he lacked physical control over his speed. He caused more harm than good. It wasn't enough to be given the gift of this power, he needed to build muscle memory and control. At this point his motivation was simple. He wanted to make use of his power but first needed to gain control.

He knew he was uniquely positioned to help his city from the perils of evil forces. Holding to that vision was important, yet his initial goal was to exercise control over his speed. Barry was clear on his motivation both short-term and longer-term. And so, his journey began.

In closing out this chapter, let's summarize the main takeaways.

Insights–What Did You Learn?

- Physical force is more concerned with external factors and how it creates the energy needed to balance our well-being.
- When we can make physical force routines a habit, we amplify their benefits and our impact.
- Endeavor to continually push past your own personal best. When you reach your goals, ask yourself "what now?"
- When we are at our best, it's externally noticeable. We physically "SHINE."
- To "SHINE":
  - Get the right amount of quality Sleep.
  - Stay Hydrated.
  - Continually Inspect your physical health.
  - Nourish your body with the right foods and habits.
  - Prioritize and build a routine for daily Exercise.
- Know what motivates you in order to remain committed and accountable to your physical force goals.

---·⚡·---

Chapter Six:
Social Force

By now you have realized that there is no exclusivity to each of the five forces. They are interconnected to form the basis of the entire makeup of the perfectly imperfect hero leader within.

In this chapter, we will explore the concepts that influence us through social engagement and interactions. How these influences manifest and take hold can either drive us forward with true purpose and motivation or hold us back due to a sense of duty in certain social settings. There's a professional and personal element to social energy, although the choices you make on how you will show up in different social settings are centered around a few factors:

1) Your personality type and traits
2) Your preferred mode of communication
3) Your engagement preferences
4) Your values
5) Your motivations

Think of these factors as the source inputs that directly influence how you show up in any personal or professional social situation. Social situations can span a variety of settings (in person, virtual—visual, virtual—auditory, social media), and they can be formal or informal.

Let's start by digging into the main factors that form the foundation of our social force.

Personality

In my 2022, interview with business owner and leader, Adam Cohen, he recounts how his parents influenced and shaped his approach in different social settings. He speaks of the subtle undertones of how they encouraged him to strive to do his best and focus on what he wanted his path to be.

It was never about the result but more about the journey to find himself, his passions, and his true purpose. Failure was expected along this journey, leading him to take confident risks in life choices that society might otherwise deem unusual and possibly unwise. Who he has become, and the choices he has made to either lean into social norms or chart a new path to society's expected norms are in large part due to his parents.

He says, (Cohen, 2022) "I never felt pressure for grades; they never questioned any of that, but there was always this subtle goal to be successful. To do what you needed to get to your goals. They were always just very supportive, and they built this environment where it was okay to lose if you tried, and if you try hard enough, you get there. It's what you learn and how you turn that around to win the next time."

With that courage, self-belief, conviction toward goals, and purpose, Adam set a standard for himself to rise above the perceived expectations of others and social norms, and make choices that fit his personality, desires, and goals. To that end, Adam embarked on three incredible life-changing events, all within a three-month span. At the age of twenty-six, Adam got married, bought a house, and opened a business.

Adam describes his commitment to his family, lifestyle, and business goals as his foundation to success. (Cohen, 2022) "You must have confidence inside and confidence of what you build and what's around you. That's your foundation. You cannot grow on a cracked foundation. Your foundation has to be strong and if your foundation is strong, then it's amazing the things that you can grow and the things you can do on it. If your foundation is cracked and you try to grow, you put more pressure on the whole thing, and it crumbles."

Most of us may not be aware of our personality traits and what impact that has on us and our social energy. The most commonly known personality type assessment is that of Myers-Briggs and has been used worldwide for decades. The personality types are defined by four elements. To get to the personality preference for you, the assessment takes you through a series of questions that require you to make a choice between two opposing information aspects.

The eight information aspects are categorized as: extraversion (E), sensing (S), thinking (T), judgment (J), introversion (I), intuition (N), feeling (F), perception (P). These categories are otherwise known as the "Socionics theory."

Socionics predicts the characteristics of individuals in given social situations and are grouped into sixteen types of personalities that each contain four of the eight elements described above.

I'll be honest, all these letters and groupings is a little overwhelming to me. I get anxious just trying to remember it all and, as a result, have difficulty recalling the relevant information for myself and how to use it. That's just me. I like simple and intuitive, and this makes me feel like I'm back at school struggling to memorize the periodic table. Nevertheless, I do think it is an interesting exercise to tune in to your personality and characteristics that drives your thinking, actions, and behaviors. Let the tool do the science and focus in on the results and what you can learn from that.

If you are wondering what my Myers-Briggs is, then never fear, I will happily share. For those who know me well, I think you'll agree it's pretty accurate. So here it is—I'm an ENFP—described as an "imaginative motivator." My summary reads (Briggs. 2022):

Extraversion | Intuition | Feeling | Perceiving
"ENFPs are enthusiastic innovators, always seeing new possibilities in the world around them. Their world is full of possible projects or interests they want to pursue. Imaginative, high-spirited, and

ingenious, they are often able to do almost anything that interests them. They are confident, spontaneous, and flexible, and often rely on their ability to improvise. They value home, family, friendships, creativity, and learning."

A whole splatter of words describes certain traits that are my strengths. I've highlighted the top characteristics that popped from my answers:

Curious, Imaginative, **Creative,** *Innovative, Insightful,* **Perceptive,** *Sociable, Gregarious, Cooperative, Supportive, Warm, Caring, Friendly, Personable,* **Enthusiastic,** *Energetic,* **Spontaneous,** *Lively, Adaptable, Versatile.*

The last part of my assessment summarizes how I engage with others personally and professionally based on the assessment results. Again, it's pretty accurate and super intriguing, given my passion with executive and leadership coaching. It highlights the strengths of engaging with others to provide insights that encourage them to see greater opportunity and potential in themselves, adaptable to different thoughts, values, and culture, and creating a sense of harmony and trust.

I find this fascinating as I think about the paths I have taken, the choices I have made, the environments I choose to engage with, and the career choices where I have thrived the most. My thirst for seeking out new possibilities, leaning into discomfort with the expected promise of adventure and innovation, feeds my heightened sense of curiosity. I am a strong believer in the continual transformation of the self, others, and things. There is always a better way.

Why do I share this? Because understanding your preferences and leading characteristics will help you better connect to where you place your social energy. Are you positioning yourself to optimize or drain yourself? Knowing your strengths and your blind spots will elevate your impact through your social engagements, whether formal, informal, personal, or professional.

A recent client of mine was thrilled at an unexpected promotion. It was a moment of clarity for her, and it gave her a boost of confidence that she had previously suppressed. Despite her successes, she found it hard to let go of self-doubt, and this promotion provided that validation through which she could release that self-doubt. But just as she did, another emotion arose with the prospect of an in-person celebration event.

She began to worry about how she might show up in this social setting. Might people judge her and think her unworthy of the reward of her promotion? What would she say when people congratulated her? What would she wear? What might she encounter that she's ill-prepared for? How should she address others celebrating their promotion? Her questions just kept coming, and anxiety was rising quickly.

It wasn't that she didn't know the answer to all of her questions; she did. Once we had worked to explore that, she realized the real concern was with the social setting.

She's an introvert with core values that cause her to avoid such events. It drains her, but at the same time, she recognized that she wanted to celebrate her achievements, and she was looking forward to seeing a couple of people whom she knew and respected. She wanted to congratulate them for their accomplishments, too.

She had spent so much energy focused on the perceived expectations of how others would want her to show up in that social setting she'd forgotten to focus on what was important to her, what she wanted to get out of attending the event.

Through surfacing this self-awareness, she changed her perception of attending this event. She became excited. Instead of thinking about this social engagement as a drain on her, she started to feel a build-up of energy toward seeing old colleagues and celebrating a moment to be proud of. She, in essence, narrowed into a smaller sphere of engagement to just those she was excited to see.

Suddenly, the prospect of being in a large crowd with many people she didn't know was no longer a daunting event. She realized she was in control of her choices. She connected with a few folks ahead of the event and made plans to meet earlier.

When they met, they shared how they each had similar anxiety. The shared vulnerability created a closer bond and a sense of security and safety. Together they were stronger. The night was a success, with new memories and connections made.

I share this example because managing your social force does not mean shying away from social engagements that cause you anxiety but rather inspecting and exploring what is behind the anxiety first. Is the anxiety driven by thinking you need to meet others' perceived expectations or live up to a standard of social etiquette that is far from your comfort levels or counter to your values? If so, then you can change that.

Determine for yourself what you want to gain from the event. What is your comfort zone? Is it about what you prefer to wear, who you know, what conversations you are curious to have, and what you may learn? Make your decision based on what you're motivated by and not what you think is the expectation, and you will find your social energy force will work in your favor rather than against you.

There are situations when avoidance can be your best strategy to maintain optimal social energy. Your parents used to warn you about these, using terms like "you don't want to fall in with the wrong crowd," "he/she's not good for you," or "you don't seem like yourself when you're around them." Okay, so your parents didn't always get it right, but you secretly knew when they were.

In many cases, we have a choice of who we engage, where, when, and to what extent. I haven't met one person yet who doesn't have certain individuals who they feel discomfort around or get overwhelmed by stress, doubt, and anxiety either during or after being in their presence.

Sometimes, it can be someone you like in other settings, but certain settings have them show up differently, causing you to feel out of sorts, or their energy draws from you somehow, leaving you low or exhausted. If you can't avoid these encounters, brief the interactions and focus on the necessary engagement with a clear purpose. Always be genuinely yourself, pointing your energy toward that which brings you excitement and constructive, positive energy.

Exercise: Exploring Social Settings—Draining or Energizing?

Introduction:

This self-discovery exercise will help you explore how different social settings affect your energy levels. By reflecting on your experiences, you can better understand which social environments drain or energize you. This exercise will involve self-reflection, observation, and analysis. Find a quiet and comfortable space where you can focus without distractions. Grab a pen and paper or open a document to record your thoughts and observations.

Step 1: Reflect on Past Experiences

Take a few moments to reflect on various social settings you have encountered in the past. Consider different scenarios such as parties, networking events, family gatherings, or one-on-one conversations. Write down the settings that come to mind and briefly describe your experiences in each.

Step 2: Identify Draining and Energizing Factors

Now, go through the list of social settings you wrote down and identify the factors that made each experience draining or energizing for you. Consider aspects such as the number of people present, the level of noise, the type of activities, the level of engagement required, and the overall atmosphere. Write down these factors next to each social setting.

Step 3: Analyze Patterns

Review the factors you identified and look for patterns or commonalities. Do you notice any consistent themes or similarities between the draining or energizing experiences? For example, you might find that large crowds drain your energy, while intimate conversations energize you. Write down any patterns or observations you discover.

Step 4: Assess Your Energy Levels

Think about how you typically feel before, during, and after different social settings. Consider your energy levels, mood, and overall well-being. Rate each experience on a scale of one to ten, with one being extremely draining and ten being highly energizing. Write down your ratings next to each social setting.

Step 5: Experiment and Observe

Now that you have identified patterns and assessed your energy levels, it's time to experiment. Attend different social settings intentionally, focusing on those that align with your energizing factors. Take note of how you feel before, during, and after each experience. Observe any changes in your energy levels, mood, or overall well-being. Write down your observations and compare them to your previous experiences.

Step 6: Reflect and Adjust

Reflect on your observations and consider how they align with your initial expectations. Are there any surprises or unexpected findings? Based on your reflections, adjust your approach to social settings accordingly. Seek out environments that energize you and limit exposure to draining ones whenever possible.

Conclusion:

This self-discovery exercise gave you valuable insights into how social settings can drain or energize you. Use this newfound knowledge to make intentional choices about the social environments you engage in. Remember, it's essential to prioritize your well-being and surround yourself with settings that bring out the best in you. Also, remember to challenge your thinking to help you better step into uncomfortable settings by reframing your own motivation and positioning.

Communication:

Your preferred communication style can be influenced by your personality and other social force factors. I've found a few things to be generally true through my research and observations.

Firstly, our communication styles shift and change depending on the audience or setting. Social norms generally dictate. We are at our most authentic selves when we are at home and surrounded by family and close friends. There is less considered or proper flow to how we communicate. There is a higher propensity for hurtful comments and heated moments. Conversely, more loving sentiments and biased opinions are shared. It's an interesting dynamic open to larger swings and a broader spectrum of emotional connection within our communication styles.

In more formal and open social settings, we tend to be narrower in our sphere of emotional connection, more guarded, and considerate of what communication is best fitting for the situation. There are often defined guardrails of what is or is not an acceptable form of communication or interaction. These guardrails or expected social norms are important and, in many cases, essential to ensure safe, ethical, and respectful engagement en masse.

As a result, our communication style adapts to meet the audience where they are. This considered approach to your communication is critical as a leader. Still, it can create a sense of inner conflict if the style best suited for an occasion is further away from your natural, preferred communication style. It can also impact your trajectory depending on your preferred or dominant communication style.

How do you remain true to your authentic self in all situations? How do you ensure whatever you are communicating is *you*? That's the real challenge! How do you embrace an outward style that fits the setting, but the undertone and currents beneath the words you use and the impression you leave are true to your core, authentic self.

A good example of this from a Marvel movie character is that of Agent Carter. Agent Peggy Carter, despite her associations with Rogers (Captain America) and heroic wartime successes, is rewarded in title only as an agent of the Strategic Scientific Reserve (SSR).

She is discriminated against for being a female and subjected to tasks only befitting of females as defined by the social norms of the late 1940s. Her male counterparts saw her as a burden or when befitting the occasion, a trophy. They each passed on their filing and administrative work to her. Nevertheless, she always found the balance to show up as expected and engage communicatively within the guardrails of her position in society while maintaining a strength and persistence to get to the right outcomes.

This marriage of choosing a communication style that's fitting of the occasion while remaining authentically you has been a tough balance for me over the years, and it takes constant work to rewire my thinking. I think it's because I'm a natural disrupter, curious about why something is the way it is, always seeing other possibilities. If I disagree with the social expectation in a particular setting, I will likely break the rules and rebel a little more than most.

Equally, my preferred communication style is emotional and linear. There are a vast variety of communication style assessments out there, and they are useful tools to help you understand what your preferences are and what that means in how you can best engage with those with either complementary or opposing preferences.

While each assessment differs in what they call something, a quadrant model is often used to define those preferences. You might also see a scale across which to measure the extent of your preferences. Regardless of what those categories are called within the quadrant models, they tend to have a similar flavor of opposing pairings.

For example, you are either more emotional/sociable or factual/analytical on one axis of the quadrant. On the other, more linear/logical or free-form/unstructured. Interestingly, the higher up in an organization you are, the more you can expect to see a bias toward the linear/logical and factual/analytical communication style preferences.

I wonder how the social force shift of the pandemic will influence a better balance and acceptance of diverse communication styles at more senior levels. In some assessments, you can even get a read on how your style can differ from your preferred style, often described as the style that shows up most in high-stress workplace situations. There is a difference in how your communication style shows up at work and socially.

It is easy to want to dive deeper into what this means to succeed as a leader when your communication style preference is at odds with the expectation within the environment you work within. But that's not where I want to go on this topic. I'd rather focus on what I discovered in my interviews with many remarkable leaders.

In my interviews with these perfectly imperfect hero leaders, their ability to find a balance between the authenticity of their preferred communication style and cultural/social expectations makes a massive difference in why they are so successful at what they do and are super inspirational to others.

I think communication styles are uniquely yours when all is said and done. Yes, there are dos and don'ts and common core communication etiquettes, but in my twenty-plus years of leading people and working within corporate America, there are a few trends that surface for me:

- *Everyone* always has some level of communication opportunity.

- There are infinite personal preferences and expectations of what good communication is.
- We all have biases toward our style and preferences of communication.
- Leaders spend too much time iterating on presentation and messaging as the material flows up the chain.
- Each level of leader has different opinions on what the ultimate audience will want to see and hear.
- It's an ineffective time suck to aim for perfection where perfection is rarely possible.
- Communications that are structured, have a clear purpose, and have validity always win the day. Donald Miller, author of, *Building a Storybrand*, would advise you to (Miller, 2017) "keep it simple" and ensure your message requires your audience to expend the "least amount of calories."
- Nerves and overthinking can make a great communicator stumble in key moments.
- Self-doubt can kill your communication impact.
- Quiet the negative self-talk and elevate the positive talk.

As I consider my research further, I have become more curious about the true impact of communication. What I have found is that there is no real correct answer. Highly successful leaders can span the full range of communication competencies. What is always true is that their communication "flaws" (if you consider there is such a thing), are accepted and seem to have limited impact on their most game-changing successes. Why is that? Here's what I found:

1) They know they have communication challenges but choose not to dwell on them as a general rule.
2) They all maximize a compensating superpower that overshadows any communication flaws.
3) They reserve the polish and command of a message for critical moments—they rehearse—they get help.
4) They know their stuff—they can handle practically any impromptu situation.
5) They set clear, bold goals and they are laser-focused on driving toward succeeding—this helps them in being confident with their communications.

Why then do we spend so much time obsessing over perfection in how we communicate? It all stems from our human instinct to comply with social expectations and for acceptance. To a certain extent, it is important to have some manner of consistency with how we engage with each other effectively. When we over index on seeking perfection, though, we can lose sight of our goals and what's important. Pursuit to perfection becomes a distraction. Important goals fail to be met or take much longer than originally anticipated. We can find ourselves justifying the outcome: "The goal never made sense," "the landscape changed so we needed to revisit the goal, rescope the outcomes."

In reality, the landscape did change, but only because timelines exploded due to overthinking the communication and paying less deliberate attention to what was needed and what it would take. The knock-on impacts continue and the justifications you give yourself and each other become acceptable. Great leaders avoid this pattern because they are less concerned with conforming to the social norm, and more concerned with forging a new way forward. If they find themselves in a setting where they are too confined to certain guardrails, they either lead the change or move to where they can be more effective. Keep this in mind as you complete the following exercise.

Exercise: Unleashing Your Communication Power

Introduction:

This exercise is designed to help you explore and establish your communication power. Effective communication is a crucial skill that can positively impact various aspects of your life. By understanding and harnessing your communication power, you can enhance your relationships, influence others, and achieve your goals. This exercise will involve self-reflection, practice, and self-assessment. Find a quiet and comfortable space where you can focus without distractions. Have a pen and paper or a document ready to record your thoughts and observations.

Step 1: Reflect on Your Communication Style

Take a few moments to reflect on your communication style. Consider how you typically express yourself, both verbally and nonverbally. Think about your strengths and areas for improvement. Write down your reflections, noting specific examples or situations that come to mind.

Step 2: Identify Your Communication Goals

Define your communication goals. What do you want to achieve through effective communication? It could be building stronger relationships, expressing yourself assertively, becoming a better listener, or influencing others positively. Write down your goals, ensuring they are specific, measurable, achievable, relevant, and time-bound (SMART goals).

Step 3: Analyze Your Strengths and Weaknesses

Analyze your strengths and weaknesses as a communicator. Consider aspects such as clarity, active listening, empathy, body language, tone of voice, and adaptability. Write down your strengths and weaknesses, providing examples or anecdotes to support your assessment.

Step 4: Enhance Your Communication Skills

Choose one or two areas of communication that you would like to improve. It could be something you identified as a weakness or an area you believe would significantly enhance your communication power. Research effective techniques, strategies, or resources related to your chosen area(s) of improvement. Take notes on these techniques and strategies.

Step 5: Practice and Observe

Put your newfound knowledge into practice. Engage in conversations or situations where you can apply the techniques and strategies you learned. Pay close attention to your communication style, body language, tone, and the reactions of others. Observe how your communication power evolves and note any changes or improvements you notice.

Step 6: Seek Feedback

Seek feedback from trusted individuals in your life, such as friends, family members, or colleagues. Ask them to provide honest feedback on your communication skills, specifically focusing on the areas you have been working on. Take note of their observations and suggestions for improvement.

Step 7: Reflect and Adjust

Reflect on your practice sessions, observations, and the feedback you received. Consider what worked well and what areas still need improvement. Adjust your approach and continue practicing enhancing your communication power further. Remember that effective communication is an ongoing process of growth and development.

Conclusion:

By completing this exercise, you have taken significant steps toward establishing and enhancing your communication power. Remember to continue practicing, seeking feedback, and refining your skills. Effective communication can empower you to connect with others, express yourself confidently, and achieve your goals. Embrace your communication power and use it to create positive and meaningful interactions in all areas of your life. Be intentional about your actions and ensure caution to avoid over perfection, which can lead to diminishing returns on your investment.

Engagement

Most major organizations measure engagement scores as part of assessing human force satisfaction. It got me thinking about what it really means to be engaged, and how might this differ for each individual. Is there a socially accepted or expected norm for someone to be "engaged?"

Who defines the bar or aspects from which to measure good or excellent engagement? Is there a common understanding across various organizations and industries? Or does each organization make its own definitions?

What might I find if I researched it in depth? On each end of the spectrum, it might reveal that there is a common understanding or that it differs, but then what? I feared I might keep searching down rabbit holes only to discover flaws in the theory across the spectrum.

Instead, I investigated what "engagement" means to different people to see if consistent themes pop up. When reading through various studies on the topic, some common words show up:

- Included
- Informed
- Valued
- Inspired
- Motivated
- Empowered
- Energized
- Recognized
- Encouraged
- Supported

To add to the above list, there is a sense of genuine interest toward fostering, building, and supporting individuals and teams, as well as personal and professional goals.

When speaking with individuals in my network across various industries, there was a psychological element toward things that mattered most to them regarding engagement:

Safety and trust; a judgment-free environment; acceptance of differences; willingness to meet them where they are; respect and acknowledgment for different cultural backgrounds, values, and beliefs and how that shows up in how they engage with the work and others. How they like to be rewarded, recognized, or included. Understanding the whole person and allowing flexibility.

The 2020 pandemic has elevated these psychological dynamics, and for many industries that have now shifted to more hybrid or remote working environments, these types of topics in the workplace are less taboo. For the first time, we are having more transparent and vulnerable conversations.

Phrases like "you need to leave your personal life out of the workplace" is now understood to be an unnatural expectation. Working from home for many has naturally blurred the lines between home and work, but most importantly, it has elevated recognition that what happens outside of work impacts how you show up at work. We give each other more space and grace to be flexible in that balance.

We have all needed to adapt to a new normal, but I find we still try to measure the same things in the same way, with some add-ons in consideration of the importance of diversity, inclusion, equity, and belonging. These important factors of diversity, inclusion, equity, and belonging are a big part of engagement. Still, most organizations continue to measure engagement against the same questions/factors as true before the 2020 pandemic and, in many cases, for the past few decades.

I invite leaders to explore your definition of engagement and study if that meets the bar for your human force. Is there a new definition unfolding? Are you measuring against the right set of questions to know how well you are doing on this dimension?

On the flip side of this, and regardless of the bar for measurement, I'm super curious about the depth of psychological factors and their impact on our energy. When we seek safety and trust rather than feeling it in the environment around us, our energy is pointed toward the pursuit of finding it.

Equally, in the meantime, we set up a shield to guard us from falling foul to the potential of being wrong, looking stupid, seeming misinformed, seeming anything other than what you think is expected.

You start assessing the characters in the room. Notice I said characters and not people. You start to give them labels: "the know it all," "the leader," "the smart one," "the creative one," "the clueless one." Somewhere in that characterization process, you start to wonder who's assessing you and what category they placed you in.

Naturally, you assume the worst—the smart one thinks you're clueless. In all this time, while you are protecting yourself in a way that helps you feel safe, you have expended a massive amount of energy that, quite frankly, has done nothing but leave you out on a limb. You've somewhat distanced yourself to the point that it's now difficult to be trusted or to trust. Was that really where you wanted your energy to be pointed? Do you have anything left in the tank to do the work needed to be a part of the whole? Whatever the whole is.

We spend so much of our social force energy pointed toward protection, self-preservation, and being accepted that we make it hard to engage effectively. This is the natural human instinct. Whether you are an extrovert, introvert, or somewhere in between, you can't escape this force of nature in what it means to be human. It just shows up differently.

Let's look at our Marvel heroes. For Thor, it shows up with humor and bravery to mask any insecurities. The Hulk shows up in swings of isolation and extreme anger. For Captain America it's self-assurance to stand at the front and lead, protected by having a clear set of plans, rules, and direction.

Even with these protective shields, it doesn't stop these hero leaders from stepping into and engage with the matter at hand, but it can and does block their ability to "see" others and "invite" them in to fully contribute to the task at hand.

No way does Captain America want the reckless actions of Iron Man to counter his well-thought-out plans. People will get hurt. Remember how I explained how we looked around the room and started to label people and categorize them into certain characteristics? I expect here's how that might go for any engagement with Captain America and Iron Man:

Iron Man's mind bubble about Capital America would read something like, "he's all muscles and no brain. All he does is follow orders. Is he capable of pivoting in the moment? I don't think so." Given that Captain America's role is to lead others into danger—what's the likelihood that Iron Man is going to feel safe and trust him? I'd say it's slim to none.

Let's reverse this. Captain America's mind bubble of Iron Man would read something like, "he has no sense of order. He cares for no one else but himself. He sits behind fancy theoretical data with no regard for how to make it work in practice. He's dangerous." Being part of the same team, to succeed in a mission, what's the likelihood that Captain America will trust Iron Man to follow his orders and keep others safe? Again, I'd say it's slim to none.

Well, the reality is they are often on the same team and while they deliver results, the journey to get there feels disjointed, clunky, and more mistakes than are necessary are made along the way. They can outwardly celebrate with each other, but when it comes to feeling "engaged" I would expect a few things show up:

- There is little trust and sense of safety.
- They feel useful in their own right, but not totally valued or included in the whole.
- It feels uncomfortable and harder than it needs to be.
- They feel obstructed, misunderstood, lonely.

The list is endless. It shows more than surface-level needs, but that deep psychological engagement is critical to perform at our best.

As perfectly imperfect hero leaders, it is your role to set the environment that gets below the surface and allows all individuals to comfortably be part of the whole. There are three words that should have stood out to you in that sentence: "all," "comfortably," and "whole".

Just ruminating on those three words will likely elevate why it is super difficult to lead others and organizations. It's a massive responsibility that takes continuous work, reflection, and more work. Consider what my research provides insight into when completing the following exercise.

Exercise: Unleashing Employee Engagement: Discovering Your Leadership Approach

Introduction:

This exercise is designed to help leaders explore and determine the best approach to foster fully engaged employees. Employee engagement is crucial for productivity, satisfaction, and overall organizational success. By understanding your leadership style and its impact on employee engagement, you can create a work environment that motivates and empowers your team. This exercise will involve self-reflection, observation, and analysis. Find a quiet and comfortable space where you can focus without distractions. Have a pen and paper or a document ready to record your thoughts and observations.

Step 1: Reflect on Your Leadership Style

Take a few moments to reflect on your leadership style. Consider how you typically lead and interact with your team members. Think about your strengths and areas for improvement as a leader. Write down your reflections, noting specific examples or situations that come to mind.

Step 2: Define Employee Engagement

Define what employee engagement means to you. Consider the behaviors, attitudes, and outcomes that indicate a fully engaged employee. Write down your definition, ensuring it aligns with your organization's goals and values.

Step 3: Assess Current Employee Engagement

Assess the current level of employee engagement within your team or organization. Consider factors such as productivity, morale, communication, collaboration, and overall satisfaction. Use surveys, feedback, or performance indicators to gather data on employee engagement. Analyze the results and identify any trends or areas of concern.

Step 4: Identify Engagement Drivers

Identify the key drivers of employee engagement within your organization. These drivers could include factors such as clear communication, recognition, growth opportunities, work-life balance, or a positive work culture. Write down the drivers you identify and rank them in order of importance based on your organization's context.

Step 5: Analyze Your Leadership Approach

Analyze how your leadership approach aligns with the identified engagement drivers. Consider whether your current style supports or hinders employee engagement. Reflect on how you communicate, motivate, empower, and support your team members. Write down your observations and note any areas where adjustments may be needed.

Step 6: Seek Employee Feedback

Seek feedback from your team members regarding their perception of your leadership style and its impact on their engagement. Conduct one-on-one meetings, focus groups, or anonymous surveys to gather honest feedback. Ask specific questions about their level of engagement, areas where they feel supported or unsupported, and suggestions for improvement. Take note of their responses and insights.

Step 7: Reflect and Adjust

Reflect on your self-reflection, analysis, and the feedback you received from your team members. Consider what changes or adjustments you can make to enhance employee engagement. Develop an action plan that outlines specific steps you will take to align your leadership approach with the identified engagement drivers. Set measurable goals and timelines to track your progress.

Conclusion:

By completing this exercise, you have taken significant steps toward determining the best approach to fully engage employees. Remember that employee engagement is a continuous effort that requires ongoing reflection, observation, and adjustment. Embrace your role as a leader and use your insights to create a work environment that fosters motivation, satisfaction, and productivity. Empower your team members, communicate effectively, and prioritize the drivers of engagement to unleash the full potential of your employees and drive organizational success.

Values:

Our values run deep. They morph and change over time to be more firmly ingrained in our outward characteristics and dictate how we make choices. We explored some of this earlier in the book to a certain extent. In this chapter, I want to take it a step further. Where exactly do our values come from?

A simple google search will bring you to an array of examples and definitions. The one that I like the most is "the regard that something is held to deserve; the importance, worth, or usefulness of something" (Oxford Languages, 2023).

I love this definition the most because it speaks to effort and experience. There is an undertone of the need to:

- Be deserving.
- Be worthy of . . .
- Be useful.
- Be important.

What this above list means to me can be very different from what it means to someone else. Our upbringing and experiences in life, or simply what we have been exposed to through media outlets, help shape the definition of each word.

My own upbringing taught me never to expect something in return for the effort given. Do something because it's the right thing to do, because it means something to someone else, to have pride in knowing, no matter what, you gave your best.

In my university days, I took a night job for a direct marketing firm for a couple of weeks. My shift started at 9 p.m. and ended at 4 a.m. I was stuffing envelopes with letters and inserts. It wasn't the most motivating or inspiring work, but I understood the purpose for getting it right, and I made sure I was clear on the goal of how many I completed within a certain time period.

I quickly found my rhythm and completed twice the volume with a 100 percent quality rating in the allotted time. This provided me with a sense of achievement and pride for doing the best I could. I didn't get paid any more for doing twice as much as everyone else, and I didn't expect to.

Consequently, I also felt like an outsider from most others, as they gave me a hard time for making them "look bad." Their focus was to only do as much as was needed and no more. Why? Because to do more came with no reward. They also feared that I was demonstrating that more was possible, and they didn't want to do more than they had been comfortable doing.

I remember feeling sad for them. That they couldn't find joy and gratitude from doing more without first receiving a reward. They were all capable of producing a lot more. For me that was bizarre. Surely, working unsociable hours and doing repetitive work was more taxing if you take your time. If you increased the pace, time would go quicker, and you could build self-motivation to get through the shift by making it more challenging. Set yourself a bigger goal and feel pride in achieving it.

At the end of the shift, I had visibly more energy than the rest of the workers and had the ability to engage and help others clear down their space, ready for the next shift to start. I was almost always the only one that greeted and took time to welcome folks on the next shift. I remember thinking "why do they think they deserve this job?"

There were so many other, more deserving people out there. This experience further ingrained a core value in me, to always strive to do your best without expectation of a reward. It also ingrained the value of earning your right to deserve a seat at the table. It's better to give than to receive.

Over my years in leadership, I have also learned to appreciate that those who don't share these same values are just as worthy as I am for a seat at the table. Their experiences have ingrained different values in them and have equally helped them grow and achieve. Having said that, I also observe a value-based expectation in different social settings within and outside of the workplace. Talk about complex.

There are so many things we must remember and adapt to in order to be included and accepted, that it can be overwhelming and difficult to keep up. It's exhausting. Each time we shift our position, we move farther away from showing up authentically and at our best. Think about that.

There are so many unintended consequences. It makes it hard for people to know what you stand for. Who you are. What they can trust in you for. It's confusing. How often as a leader do you have to put your values aside to do what is expected by the company? The way in which you approach that situation can be damaging to your credibility and the trust your team has in you. You must be mindful of the audience and to what extent you expose that conflict but maintain an appreciation for all ranges of perspective. Finding balance is hard but necessary.

The alternative is to position yourself in an organization where everyone aligns to the same values and core beliefs. In this situation, you now face narrower perspectives, less challenge, and therefore less growth as individuals, teams, and as an organization.

Interestingly, those who seek out comfort over challenge are also those that highly value security in their role. Unfortunately, this is rarely a match made in heaven. If the company doesn't grow and profits dry out, so does the security of the job you feel so comfortable in.

To face challenges, to face conflict, brings curiosity, and from curiosity comes growth and inspiration. As a result, if you want to be your best, I'd encourage you to surround yourself with those less like you. It's from this position that you elevate your social force.

Like with most other topics we have explored in this book so far, differences are less about what you see on the surface, but more so to do with what lies deep within. This is where it is so important to invite the vulnerability to better understand the values of others and where they come from.

When taking my formal training to be an executive and leadership coach, Valorie Burton introduced me to a values-based assessment, developed by the father of positive psychology Martin Seligman. Valorie studied under Seligman and had a deep understanding of how meaningful it is to connect to your highest personal value and equally understand and appreciate the top values that others hold. The assessment is called "Values in Action" (VIA).

You can find this assessment on the positive psychology page of the University of Pennsylvania's website. The website describes the assessment as follows (VIA. 2005):
"The Values in Action (VIA) Survey of Character Strengths is a 240-item face-valid self-report questionnaire . . . reflecting the 24 strengths of character that comprise the VIA Classifications."

Valorie encourages you to identify your top five of the twenty-four strengths. Again, I am happy to share what my top five are:

1. Forgiveness and mercy (always forgive, give second chances; principle of mercy, not revenge).
2. Fairness, equity, and justice (treat people fairly; personal feelings tend not to bias your decisions about others. Give everyone a chance).
3. Creativity, ingenuity, and originality (thinking of new ways of doing things, not content with doing things the conventional way, if there is a better way).
4. Citizenship, teamwork, and loyalty (excel as a member of a group; work hard for the success of the group).
5. Capacity to love and be loved (value close relationships, where sharing and caring are reciprocated).

You can immediately see from the language used that these are value-based words that connect to psychological states of being. There is emotion behind the words.

The Power of Values in Action

Earlier in this book, when exploring our mental force, I introduced you to the idea of how the way we feel influences how we think and, in turn, the actions we take. Here's why I love the VIA so much. It taps into feelings and emotions first. It's the natural, human starting point that leads to how we show up in any given situation.

When my feelings are triggered by an event where I feel wronged, my instinct is to give the benefit of the doubt and open up my thinking to see the other person's point of view.

I'm willing and able to hear their position and regardless of whether I agree or not, I'm able to move forward. Why? Because it's my top value to show mercy and forgive, so even in the most disappointing situation, I can show up in the most measured and resilient way.

If, however, the way in which either myself or someone else is wronged is due to an unfair, unjust, or unethical act, I'm less adaptable to the measured thinking. I sit with the emotions much longer and may over index to ensure appropriate action is taken. Even then, I'm likely to let the emotions linger and morph into anger and then sadness.

It's in these moments that I am now more aware of what is needed to move forward constructively. I look at my list of five top values, and there is always one that will help me pull myself forward with constructive, optimistic thoughts and actions. In this scenario, I might turn to the love and care of others to help me with where I'm sitting with my emotions. From there, I will likely turn to my core value of creativity and seek to drive a better way to address the unfair situation productively.

In all my research, I have discovered that perfectly imperfect hero leaders intuitively connect to theirs and others' core values in powerful ways to make big things happen. It's an art that requires deliberation and meaningful attention. It's centered around the hero that lies within. One that considers the whole from all perspectives to achieve overall comfort with the outcome.

Exercise: Leading with Values: Exploring Personal and Team Values

Introduction:

This exercise is designed to help leaders explore their own values and the values of their team members. Understanding and aligning personal and team values is crucial for effective leadership and fostering a balanced and considered approach. By gaining clarity on values, leaders can create a work environment that respects and supports the diverse perspectives and motivations of their team members. This exercise will involve self-reflection, team engagement, and analysis. Find a quiet and comfortable space where you can focus without distractions. Have a pen and paper or a document ready to record your thoughts and observations.

Step 1: Reflect on Your Personal Values

Take a few moments to reflect on your personal values. Consider what is most important to you in your personal and professional life. Think about the principles, beliefs, and qualities that guide your decision-making and behavior. Write down your reflections, noting specific examples or situations demonstrating your values in action. Alternatively, take the "Values in Action" VIA assessment offered through the University of Pennsylvania's website. Write down your top five values.

Step 2: Identify Team Values

Engage with your team members to identify their values. (You may choose to have them take the University of Pennsylvania VIA survey of character strengths assessment as a starting point.) Conduct individual or group discussions where team members can openly share their values. Encourage them to reflect on what matters most to them and how their values influence their work. Create a safe and inclusive space for open dialogue and active listening. Take notes on the values expressed by each team member.

Step 3: Analyze Commonalities and Differences

Analyze the values expressed by both you and your team members. Look for commonalities and differences among the values identified. Consider how these values align or diverge from each other. Reflect on the potential impact of these values on team dynamics, collaboration, and overall performance. Write down your observations and insights.

Step 4: Assess Alignment with Organizational Values

Assess the alignment of personal and team values with the organization's values. Review your organization's stated values and compare them to those identified by yourself and your team members. Consider whether there is congruence or potential areas of tension. Reflect on how the alignment or misalignment of values may impact team motivation, engagement, and overall success. Write down your assessment. Consider doing this as a team also.

Step 5: Facilitate Value-Based Discussions

Facilitate value-based discussions within your team. Create a structured forum where team members can openly share their values, discuss their importance, and explore how they can be integrated into the team's work. Encourage respectful dialogue and active listening. Seek to find common ground and shared values to guide the team's actions and decision-making. Take note of the insights and agreements reached during these discussions.

Step 6: Develop a Values-Based Leadership Approach

Develop a values-based leadership approach based on the insights gained from personal and team values. Consider how you can incorporate and honor the shared values within your leadership style and team practices. Identify specific actions and behaviors that demonstrate your commitment to these values. Create a plan to communicate and reinforce these values within the team.

Step 7: Reflect and Adjust

Reflect on your self-reflection, team engagement, and the insights gained throughout this exercise. Consider how your understanding of personal and team values has evolved and how it can inform your leadership approach. Adjust your actions and behaviors accordingly, ensuring they align with the shared values of your team and organization. Continuously reflect on and refine your approach to maintain a balanced and considered leadership style.

Conclusion:

By completing this exercise, you have taken significant steps toward exploring personal and team values to better lead your team in a balanced and considered way. Remember that values are dynamic and may evolve over time. Continuously engage with your team members, foster open dialogue, and adapt your leadership approach to honor the shared values within your team. By leading with values, you can create a work environment that respects and supports your team members' diverse perspectives and motivations, ultimately driving team success and organizational growth.

Motivation

We have just explored how our values are at the forefront of driving our thoughts and actions. It's deeply rooted in who we are, based on our values. Motivation sits on the shoulders of our core values and further amplifies a leader's impact.

Motivation is what gives meaning to our purpose. These are the facets of our life that serve to inspire us, stimulate our senses, drive purposeful outcomes, propel us toward certain actions, and help to define our purpose.

Motivation is an important driving force behind how we present ourselves in social settings, what we engage in, and what we choose to sit on the sidelines for. Like with other important factors that help us function at our best, other forces at play suck our energy into a vortex of serving someone else's agenda. Where does this all begin?

Let's start with the labels we are assigned: mother, father, sister, brother, subordinate (I hate that word—we need to change it). Then there are other types of labels based on what others see you are good at. Things like being super organized, gets shit done, solves problems.

What this means is that depending on the label and the environment you are in, the expected social norms can dictate the role you play, regardless of how well they fit with what motivates you. Your past actions and others' interpretations of those actions can overtake where you point your social energy. You find yourself in situations and wonder why I am here. What am I doing this for? And find yourself saying because I'm his sister and . . . or that's what sons do, or because my job requires it, or my boss told me to.

Usually, we stop there, accepting this as the right answer, but is it? How about you continue asking yourself these important questions? Is this where I want to be? What else could I be doing? What would it mean to do (you fill the gap)? What's stopping me from doing the things I prefer to do—things that motivate me? What is it that makes others think this is the role I want to play? How can I change that?

I have many clients who have life-changing effects when we explore these questions when they are stuck in a place where they don't know what to do next. One hundred percent of the time it's down to where they place their energy, keeping them away from the things they want to do. Keeping them away from what motivates them and, ultimately, from fulfilling their purpose.

I hear things like, "It's just not the right time." When I pause long enough to think it through, they will follow with something else like, "I really don't have the time right now." A further pause leads to what's taking up so much of their time. It generally falls into one of three categories: family, work, and social commitments.

In all cases, every individual is in control of making meaningful changes, even for things like "my family looks to me to . . ." or "it's my job to . . ." or "I committed to do this for my friend a long time ago. I can't let them down."

The way in which these clients get to figure out what needs to change is to explore their motivation. What is it that drives them? How much time do they spend pointed toward their motivations? When they really unpack this, they realize that change is necessary to move forward with purpose.

Inevitably, they will come back to "but I don't have time." Although, this time, we take a different approach. We get real. We chart recent events and dissect how they came about and what they did. Then when I ask, "and if you weren't there to do (fill the gap), what would happen?" Of course, I get the sky is falling, all hell broke loose, and the world is ending, but, eventually, there is a realization that there are other options, and in some cases, there actually have been situations when all turned out fine. So, then we look at where they are willing to start in changing people's expectations of them.

Perfectly imperfect hero leaders work hard on this. They keep in the driver's seat where they are headed and with whom. They are clear on how they choose to engage and for how long. It is all anchored toward being super clear with others on their purpose and their motivation, which in turn motivates others to help them on that journey, so when they say no or do not engage in a way that others would hope, they understand for themselves that to do this stands in between them and what they are pursuing with higher motivational force.

By now, you've realized that the social force section is where it's helpful to use self-assessment tools. They all have some measure of determining strengths. Still, I have purposefully chosen to highlight some of my favorites tied to where my research points to there being the biggest return on pointing your energy in the right direction. We looked at Myers-Briggs to elevate awareness of how your personality and certain characteristics drive you and serve you when engaging with others. We elevated awareness of your top five values and how they drive you and serve you using the VIA.

Assess Your Motivation

In this section, I want to point you toward another popular assessment tool that helps you tune in to understand what motivates you and, in turn, helps define your purpose: the CliftonStrength finder. Like with the other two assessments we've discussed, you will be guided to answer many questions, which will identify your top five strengths. I will, again, share my results to illustrate the differences each assessment will provide you and channel your focus to where they best serve you in being your best.

Here are my top five CliftonStrengths (Clifton, 2022):
1. Futuristic (inspired by the future and what it could be; inspire others with their visions of the future).
2. Maximizer (focus on strengths to stimulate personal and group excellence; they seek to transform something strong into something superb).
3. Connectedness (have faith in the links between all things: no coincidences, everything/every event has a reason).
4. Activator (can make things happen by turning thoughts into action, are often impatient).
5. Belief (certain core values that are unchanging. These values define their purpose in life).

Once again, this is accurate when considering what motivates me and what I do best. It doesn't mean I'm not good at other things. It just means when I'm not functioning in a space that aligns with my top motivations (strengths), I don't shine as brightly. My value is still highly appreciated, but my impact is somewhat limited.

Like with most powers, motivation can either fuel you to shine at your best or, when overused, be the reason for your worst failures. Let's take a lesson from Achilles, one of the greatest heroes of Greek mythology who is driven by deep motivation.

Achilles is a central character in Homer's epic poem, *The Iliad*, and he is known for his exceptional strength, bravery, and skill in battle. However, what truly drives Achilles is his overwhelming desire for glory and immortality.

Achilles is the son of the mortal King Peleus and the sea nymph Thetis. From a young age, his mother, Thetis, aware of his fate, tries to protect him by dipping him in the river Styx, making him invulnerable except for his heel, which she holds onto while dipping him. This act refers to the term "Achilles' heel," representing a person's vulnerability.

As Achilles grows older, he becomes aware of a prophecy that he will die young but will be remembered forever. This prophecy fuels his deep motivation to achieve everlasting glory. He seeks to become the greatest warrior of his time, surpassing all others in skill and valor. Achilles believes that achieving unmatched glory on the battlefield will secure his place in history and be remembered for eternity.

His motivation is tested during the Trojan War, where he fights on the side of the Greeks against the Trojans. However, his motivation is severely challenged when Agamemnon, the Greek king, takes Achilles's war prize, a maiden named Briseis, as his own. This insult deeply wounds Achilles's pride and honor, leading him to withdraw from the war and refuse to fight.

Achilles's absence from the battlefield causes the Greeks to suffer heavy losses, and his close friend Patroclus is killed by the Trojan prince Hector. Consumed by grief and rage, Achilles returns to the war, seeking revenge for Patroclus's death. He engages in a fierce battle with Hector and ultimately kills him, fulfilling his desire for vengeance.

However, Achilles's motivation for glory remains unfulfilled. He knows that his own death is imminent, and he is faced with a choice: Live a long, peaceful life but be forgotten, or die young but be remembered forever. Achilles chooses the latter, knowing that his name will be immortalized throughout history.

In the end, Achilles's deep motivation for glory and immortality drives him to achieve great feats on the battlefield but also leads to his tragic demise. His story serves as a reminder of the complex nature of human motivations and the lengths individuals may go to fulfill their deepest desires.

Exercise: Uncovering Motivation: Exploring Personal and Team Drivers

Introduction:

This exercise is designed to help leaders explore their own motivation and the motivation of their teams. Understanding the drivers fueling your own and your team members' actions and behaviors is crucial for effective leadership and fostering a motivated and engaged humanforce. By gaining insight into individual strengths and motivations, leaders can create a work environment that aligns with these drivers, increasing productivity and satisfaction. This exercise will involve self-reflection, team engagement, and the utilization of the CliftonStrengths Finder assessment tool. Find a quiet and comfortable space where you can focus without distractions. Have a pen and paper or a document ready to record your thoughts and observations.

Step 1: Reflect on Your Personal Motivation

Take a few moments to reflect on your personal motivation as a leader. Consider what drives you to excel in your role and what brings you a sense of fulfillment. Reflect on the tasks, responsibilities, or achievements that energize and inspire you. Write down your reflections, noting specific examples or situations that demonstrate your motivation in action.

Step 2: Introduce the CliftonStrengths Finder Assessment

Introduce the CliftonStrengths Finder assessment tool to your team members. Explain the purpose of the assessment, which is to identify and understand individual strengths and motivations. Share the benefits of discovering and leveraging these strengths in the workplace. Provide instructions for team members to complete the assessment online or distribute the assessment codes if already completed.

Step 3: Complete the CliftonStrengths Finder Assessment

Complete the CliftonStrengths Finder assessment yourself. Answer the questions honestly and thoughtfully to gain accurate insights into your strengths and motivations. Take note of your top strengths as identified by the assessment.

Step 4: Analyze Personal Strengths and Motivations

Analyze your personal strengths and motivations as identified by the CliftonStrengths Finder assessment. Reflect on how these strengths align with your personal motivation and leadership style. Consider how you can leverage these strengths to enhance your leadership effectiveness and drive your own motivation. Write down your observations and insights.

Step 5: Facilitate Team Discussions

Facilitate team discussions around individual strengths and motivations. Encourage team members to share their top strengths as identified by the CliftonStrengths Finder assessment. Create a safe and inclusive space for team members to discuss how these strengths align with their personal motivation and work preferences. Encourage team members to share examples of utilizing their strengths in their roles. Take note of the strengths and motivations shared by each team member.

Step 6: Identify Team Motivators

Identify common motivators within the team based on the shared strengths and motivations. Look for patterns or themes that emerge from the discussions. Consider how these motivators align with the team's goals and objectives. Reflect on leveraging these motivators to create a work environment that fosters motivation and engagement. Write down the identified team motivators.

Step 7: Develop a Motivation-Driven Leadership Approach

Develop a motivation-driven leadership approach based on the insights gained from personal and team motivators. Consider how you can align your leadership style, tasks, and responsibilities with the identified motivators. Identify specific actions and behaviors demonstrating your commitment to fostering motivation within the team. Create a plan to communicate and reinforce these motivators within the team.

Step 8: Reflect and Adjust

Reflect on your self-reflection, team engagement, and the insights gained throughout this exercise. Consider how your understanding of personal and team motivation has evolved and how it can inform your leadership approach. Adjust your actions and behaviors, ensuring they align with the shared motivators of your team. Continuously reflect on and refine your approach to maintain a motivated and engaged humanforce.

Conclusion:

By completing this exercise, you have taken significant steps toward exploring personal and team motivation to better lead your team. Remember that motivation is a dynamic force that may evolve over time. Continuously engage with your team members, foster open dialogue, and adapt your leadership approach to align with the identified motivators. By understanding and leveraging individual and team strengths, you can create a work environment that fuels motivation, productivity, and satisfaction, ultimately driving team success and organizational growth.

Insights—What Did You Learn?

Let me bring this all together for you.

1) Your social force is the powerful placement of where you spend your time to live your best life and fulfill your purpose.

2) You control where you point your energy and how you show up.

3) Social forces at play will distract you and pull you away from where you ultimately want to be at any given time.

4) It's normal not to be able to articulate your purpose, which may morph and build over time. However, you will know instinctively that things are off:

   a) Feeling more stressed rather than challenged.

   b) Low energy.

   c) Increased frustration and irritability.

d) Constantly questioning what you are doing and why.

e) Wondering why you keep getting similar types of assignments at work that, while you are good at them, aren't really that fulfilling.

f) Wondering why you're the one in the family that everyone relies on for certain things or conversely are not relied on, and you want to be.

5) You need to be deliberate in exploring where you want to point your social energy and commit to building distance from the social forces that distract you.

6) Be deliberate in letting others know what drives you and where you are headed. Sing it loud and sing it proud. If you don't, others will decide for you what they think you want based on what your past tells them you are good at. If your purpose lies in doing more of the same, then great. If not, write the "future you" script, rehearse it, promote it, believe it, perform it!

7) Develop the social network, engagements, and interactions that will take you toward your purpose. If you did a good job of #6, they'll find you. There will be an abundance of what feels like chance encounters that just happened.

8) Don't go it alone—leverage your ever-developing strategic network, use mentors, and get yourself a coach to help you get there faster and keep you on track. Use key assessment tools to help you gain clarity and build awareness for defining your purpose. These tools will help you figure out:

a) Who you are and why—Myers-Briggs.
b) What your core values are and how to maximize them—VIA.
c) What motivates you—CliftonStrengths Finder.

As I close out this chapter, I have a big question: when you consider where you are pointing your social force, how is that serving you?

---·⚡·---

Chapter Seven:
Cultural Force

The phrase "it's who you are" takes on a whole new meaning for me when I think about the opportunities, I have been afforded in my life thus far. Yes, there are some innate qualities that make us who we are, but so much is a creation of the culture we have grown up in or experienced throughout life.

I'm somewhat ashamed of my naivete as a child and young adult that I took so many things for granted because of who my parents were, where they came from, and where we lived and grew up. I considered this the base from where everyone else started, and we were all equally capable of achieving the same as everyone else in the world.

To some extent, it sparked a desire to make the most of what I had around me to do the best I could, but it gave me a narrowly focused footing as I became a leader to others. I could not fully appreciate the diversity of backgrounds, especially if we grew up in the same neighborhood, city, country.

My neighbors growing up came from a wide variety of backgrounds: British, Greek, Indian, and Irish, and my own parents grew up in Italy. I naively thought it didn't matter that we all came from different cultural backgrounds because we all lived on the same street in England, with kids all going to the same schools, working in the same community, receiving the same education, and health care benefits. As a result, we would all be afforded the same opportunities in life. We were all starting from the same starting line.

I mentioned in the previous chapter that some of my top five values are fairness, equity, and justice. This strength misguided me in my youth and most likely throughout pockets of my career. I was somewhat blinded by the reality of how cultural differences can affect an individual's ability to take their preferred path.

Only those with a high-risk tolerance, insatiable persistence, and self-belief can break through the barriers presented by cultural influences. For many, their journey is longer and harder than it should be as a result.

In some cultures, it might not be possible at all, and to do something as simple as being a girl and wanting an education can be a life-threatening move.

I'm pained by this. As a human race, worldwide we have a duty as perfectly imperfect hero leaders to lead the change. Set the standard to invite all backgrounds in and appreciate the implications of what an opportunity might mean for them in their personal life.

A few years back, I was part of a game-changing project. I was often faced with challenging situations with big problems to be resolved, often requiring technical capabilities. I am not a technical person but was surrounded by some amazing talented technical engineers and product owners. I remember continually being in awe of one of the female engineers. She had such bold thinking and creative problem-solving capabilities that not only sought to address the immediate need, but to think beyond the immediate problem and provide solutions that far advanced the initial objective. No one was listening to her. She was constantly drowned out, spoken over, and sometimes blatantly excluded from conversations.

I was astonished. Was I the only one seeing this? I made it my mission to help her voice be heard. I would call her into the conversation, and when I saw people interrupt her and shut her down, I would speak up and bring attention that she was not finished, and I was curious to hear what she had to say. I would encourage collaboration around her ideas as well as others and leveraged the expertise of other talents to bring structure to the conversations and document options. She started to gain recognition, and her ideas rose to the surface as the most effective solutions.

A year or so later, I was in a position to invite her to apply for an advancement opportunity that if successful, would increase her impact through increased responsibility. It would lead her to the next level, with higher earning potential. She was more than capable of the work itself. She had proved her ability and value time and time again, but I was taken aback by her response when I approached her about the role.

While she agreed she was capable of the role and it would be work that excited her, she could not apply. She expressed that if she were successful, this would put her at a higher salary and level than her husband, which would not be acceptable in the culture she grew up in. She loved her husband and enjoyed the traditions of her cultural heritage. The gains she would have through this career change would have devastating implications to her life outside of work; a life she loved.

For her, she had far more to gain by being great in the job and level she already assumed than to risk losing the life she loved, with the people she loved, for a better title and more money.

Value #2 was rising up in me. While I didn't verbalize my thoughts, I couldn't help feeling that it's not fair that she must accept this reality when she is capable of far more. She has just as much right to the higher-level role that any of the male folk in her family. Why was she okay with this? I couldn't ask and didn't, but I did probe to better understand what was important to her in her work.

She was truly happy with her decision and thanked me for helping her find her voice and giving her the equal platform to contribute her ideas. That was all she wanted. That's what she needed and no more. Through this experience, I gained an elevated appreciation for the cultural differences within our upbringing that have a massive influence on the choices we make or are even available to us.

I also realized that we don't all want to fight against certain traditions. In fact, our experience may be a positive one, which we are trying to preserve. I don't have to agree with it, but I do need to respect it. My point of view in this situation was missing so much context and perspective. I was seeing this purely from my perspective and assumed she *really* wanted what her culture traditionally forbade. She didn't. She continues to thrive and is immensely happy with her work and life.

I learned to listen with more curiosity from which to react without judgment and position myself as an advocate for what was important to her and not me. That's not to say that I won't continue to test the waters with some thoughtfully positioned questions from time to time, but I will begin that journey from where they stand and not from where I stand.

Leading the Change Must Consider the Shoes in Which Those You Lead Are Standing!

This was an important lesson to learn and one I wanted to share, as it provides a different perspective on what I mean by it being our duty to lead the change. That doesn't mean we assume the change that others ought to be seeking. It means we first take the time to listen and understand and move with intention from there. It also means that there is never a one-size-fits-all approach.

Consider the unintended consequences your actions can have on others when leading people. Create the environment for all cultures to thrive and shine, provide equal pathways to opportunities, bring awareness to opportunities, provide the resources to help all explore their options, and allow individuals to make choices for themselves without judgment.

There's a flip side to this story. One that is less about exclusion than the privilege of having a perceived advantage due to the culture you represent. As a British person living and working in America, I can often find my accent to be an advantage. People like to listen to me talk, and for some reason, I'm considered smart just because of my accent.

There are many things I am smart about and so many other things I am not savvy about, but nevertheless, there are occasions when, no matter the topic being discussed, people assume I have a valid point. I am super conscious of this for a couple of reasons. When people pay close attention to what you say and have a preconceived notion that you are a guru at whatever conversation is being had, it's all too easy to disappoint and invite criticism when people pay closer attention to what you say than most.

The other reason is that it provides an opportunity to help others be heard. I remember being in a meeting and we were debating a problem statement and how to address it. Lots of ideas were being thrown around. It was quite energizing. One of my male colleagues made a fantastic suggestion, but no one responded. I heard it loud and clear, and he attempted to make his point several times. Still, no one responded. For a moment

I thought maybe there was something I was missing that others had tuned in to, which made it a no-go! Then I thought, well, they should at least acknowledge what he said.

After a few more minutes of observation, I conducted an experiment by saying the exact thing he had said multiple times, and this time everyone paused and congratulated me for coming up with such a brilliant idea. Time to reveal the truth. I said, "I'd love to take the credit, but all I did was repeat what he said," pointing to my male colleague. As not to make everyone feel bad, I simply invited him into the conversation and asked him to tell us more.

The point is we all make assumptions based on people's cultural backgrounds that are often untrue. Many of my Indian friends get pigeonholed into specific types of roles, and their capabilities in other job families are immediately discounted.

Our cultural norms can also cause us to make statements that can be hurtful, while not intended, that's how they land. When I meet people for the first time and we're having that get to know each other conversation, the conversation turns to what brought me to the US from the UK. Nine times out of ten, it's approached through an assumptive statement, something along the lines of "so, did you move here with your husband's job?" I wonder why they didn't ask a less judgmental question instead, like "what brought you to the US?" To which I would respond, "My job with Capital One brought me here."

I feel a stab each time that conversation happens. Why? Because for a short while my brain wanders into unhelpful internal chatter—do I seem incapable? What does this mean about the first impression I've made? These types of questions swirl for a bit and then I shrug my shoulders and think to myself, what does it matter? I know what I'm worth and what I'm capable of and I'm proud of it, and I move on. Still, a more mindful and thoughtful consideration can and should be the new norm.

In Marvel's 2018 movie *Black Panther*, Wakanda is portrayed as an advanced African nation that has managed to keep its technological advancements hidden from the rest of the world. The cultural differences within Wakanda and its impact on the story are significant elements of the film.

1. Afrofuturism: Wakanda is deeply rooted in Afrofuturism, a cultural and artistic movement that combines African aesthetics and traditions with futuristic elements. This cultural difference is showcased through the nation's advanced technology, vibrant costumes, and architectural designs. The impact of Afrofuturism in the movie is the creation of a unique and visually stunning world that celebrates African culture and challenges traditional Western narratives.

2. Traditional vs. Modern: Wakanda presents a contrast between traditional African customs and modern advancements. The impact of this cultural difference is seen in the tension between those who advocate for preserving tradition and those who

embrace progress. This conflict is exemplified through the character of T'Challa, the Black Panther, who must navigate the expectations of his people while also considering the potential benefits and consequences of sharing Wakanda's technology with the outside world.

3. Tribalism: Wakanda is divided into different tribes, each with its own customs, beliefs, and leaders. These cultural differences are significant in shaping the political landscape of the nation. The impact of tribalism is explored through power struggles, alliances, and conflicts within Wakanda. It highlights the complexities of governance and the challenges of maintaining unity in a diverse society.

4. Pan-Africanism: While Wakanda is a fictional nation, it represents a broader concept of Pan-Africanism, which emphasizes the unity and solidarity of people of African descent worldwide. The impact of this cultural difference is reflected in the film's exploration of identity, heritage, and the responsibility Wakanda has toward the global African dispersion.

In *Wakanda Forever* these cultural differences continue to play a significant role, further exploring themes of identity, tradition, progress, and the impact of Wakanda's unique position in the world.

Let's do some further exploring of what this energy force means to you as a leader when considering cultural differences.

Unleashing the Power of Cultural Diversity

Exercise 1: Celebrating Our Differences

In this exercise, we will explore how cultural differences can be optimized within your teams, fostering an environment where every individual's unique background shines brightly. This exercise is designed to be conducted as a team activity, encouraging open dialogue, and celebrating diverse cultures.

1. Gather your team members and create a vibrant cultural fair. Encourage everyone to bring a taste of their heritage, whether it's through traditional food, music, dance, or even storytelling. Let the energy flow as you celebrate the rich tapestry of diverse backgrounds.

2. Facilitate meaningful conversations during the event. Encourage open dialogue about the various customs, traditions, and values that shape your team members' identities. Create a safe space for individuals to share personal stories highlighting how their cultural backgrounds have positively influenced their work.

3. Challenge your team to discuss how their unique perspectives have contributed to problem-solving, innovation, and creativity within your organization. Encourage them to reflect on the strengths and insights that arise from their diverse backgrounds.

4. Emphasize the importance of active listening and embracing these stories. Foster an inclusive environment where everyone feels valued and appreciated for their individuality without judgment.

The goal of this exercise is to optimize cultural differences, transforming them into powerful catalysts for growth and success. By harnessing the strength of your diverse humanforce, you can propel your organizations to new heights.

Exercise 2: Uncovering Biases and Assumptions

In this exercise, we will focus on strengthening self-awareness and identifying personal biases, judgments, and assumptions that may stand in the way of optimizing talent from diverse backgrounds. This exercise is designed to be conducted individually, allowing leaders to reflect and introspect.

1. Find a quiet space to focus and reflect without distractions. Close your eyes and take a few deep breaths, allowing yourself to relax and be present in the moment.

2. Bring to mind a recent interaction or decision involving a team member from a different cultural background. Reflect on your initial thoughts, feelings, and reactions during that moment.

3. Ask yourself: Did any biases, judgments, or assumptions arise? Were there any preconceived notions that influenced your perception or actions?

4. Take a few moments to explore the origin of these biases, judgments, or assumptions. Are they based on personal experiences, societal influences, or cultural conditioning?

5. Challenge yourself to see beyond these biases and assumptions. Consider how they may limit your ability to fully understand and appreciate the unique talents and perspectives that individuals from diverse backgrounds bring to the table.

6. Finally, commit to actively working on overcoming these biases and assumptions. Embrace a mindset of curiosity, empathy, and openness to optimize the talent within our diverse human force.

Remember, self-awareness is the first step toward growth and transformation. By acknowledging and addressing our biases, judgments, and assumptions, we can create a workplace that celebrates and leverages the full potential of every individual.

So let's embark on this journey of self-discovery and commit to optimizing talent from diverse backgrounds. Together we can create a workplace that thrives on inclusivity, understanding, and collaboration.

What this energy source is all about is the ability to place your energy around cultural differences in a way that embraces and respects traditions as well as the evolution and advancement of cultures in a way that avoids assumptions with how you engage. Ask open questions and listen carefully; observe without judgment and invite all voices in; where you have the privilege, use it to raise others and be their advocate, but don't assume privilege. Check your biases, explore new truths, build understanding and education to engage with increased impact.

Understand that we all have different starting points even when it appears we are starting on a level playing field—seek to understand where someone is starting from before advancing the conversation. When we do this, we create constructive and progressive outcomes for individuals, teams, and companies alike!

So far, we have spoken about culture in terms of country of origin or cultural heritage. Still, it's equally as important to think about the culture of any given organization that you are part of or lead within. It sets the tone for the company's brand and identity.

Company culture refers to the shared values, beliefs, attitudes, and behaviors that shape the work environment and interactions within an organization. It encompasses the company's mission, vision, goals, ethics, and the way employees collaborate and engage with one another. A strong and positive company culture can have several benefits for both the organization and its employees.

1. Employee Engagement and Satisfaction: A positive company culture fosters a sense of belonging, purpose, and pride among employees. When employees feel connected to the organization's values and goals, they are more likely to be engaged, motivated, and satisfied with their work. This, in turn, leads to higher productivity, lower turnover rates, and increased loyalty.

2. Attraction and Retention of Talent: A strong company culture can act as a magnet for top talent. When organizations have a reputation for a positive work environment, employees are more likely to be attracted to join the company. Additionally, a positive culture helps retain existing employees, reducing turnover and the associated costs of recruitment and training.

3. Collaboration and Teamwork: A healthy company culture promotes collaboration, open communication, and teamwork. When employees feel comfortable sharing ideas, seeking feedback, and working together, it enhances creativity, problem-solving, and innovation. This collaborative environment leads to better decision-making, increased efficiency, and improved overall performance.

4. Increased Productivity and Performance: A positive company culture can directly impact productivity and

performance. When employees are motivated, engaged, and aligned with the organization's values, they are likelier to go the extra mile, take ownership of their work, and strive for excellence. This results in higher productivity levels, improved quality of work, and better outcomes for the organization.

5. Enhanced Employee Well-Being: A supportive company culture prioritizes physical and mental employee well-being. Organizations that value work-life balance, provide opportunities for growth and development, and prioritized employee health and wellness create a positive and healthy work environment. This, in turn, leads to reduced stress, improved job satisfaction, and better overall well-being for employees.

6. Positive Reputation and Brand Image: A strong company culture can contribute to a positive reputation and brand image. Employees who are happy and engaged become brand ambassadors, speaking positively about their organization and its values. This positive word of mouth can attract customers, partners, and potential employees, enhancing the organization's overall reputation and brand image.

In summary, a company culture that promotes engagement, collaboration, employee well-being, and a sense of purpose can have numerous benefits. It leads to higher employee satisfaction, increased productivity, improved teamwork, better talent attraction and retention, and a positive brand image. Ultimately, a strong company culture contributes to the long-term success and sustainability of the organization.

But you knew all this already, right? So, how come so many organizations get it wrong? It comes down to the strength of their leadership. How well do the actions and values of the leader align to the promoted vision, mission, goals, and values of the organization?

When you say one thing and your "human force" experiences something different, trust and safety begin to collapse. In turn, the culture in practice begins to shift, and purpose and meaning becomes lost.

A strong culture is hard to maintain and continue to grow. Therefore, if you once had it and then lost it, it's hard to get back. As a leader, it's vital to be deliberate and intentional about driving consistent focus and actions that align with the company and team culture.

If you find yourself no longer inspired or aligned with a company's purpose, mission, and vision, there is nothing wrong with that. You must recognize that maybe the company or you have evolved to something or someone different in this next season of your life and career or business growth. Unless you are charged with correcting a dysfunctional culture within an organization or team, this might be a moment to rethink if you are at the right place doing the right thing.

Leaders often avoid self-recognition of a culture's changing tides, either in the company they work for or in themselves. They continue to justify the change and ignore the signs that surface, and, in turn, they become dissatisfied and unfulfilled.

Insights—What Did You Learn?

- Culture is so much more than a person's identity and cultural traditions.
- Our cultural heritage evolves and advances through the placement of our environment.
- Learn to lean into your curiosity to understand and learn from others with different perspectives.
- Tune in to signs that your cultural energy needs reinvestment or focus.
- Mindfully act and respond to others without judgment based on cultural assumptions.
- Stand in the shoes of those you lead to effectively lead change.
- Maintaining and growing a company or team culture requires consistently delivering what you say.
- Remain true to your values and continually assess alignment with the culture you work within.

Overall, are you personally living up to the promises you and your organization claim to live by? Are you leaving it to others to do this hard work? How are you investing in yourself and the connections in your teams to foster trust in the culture?

How are you supporting others to live the culture of the company or team you lead?

Like anything else discussed in this book, it takes continual practice, reflection, and learning to get this right. Don't assume that when you have reached the goal of building a culture that all can thrive in, it will remain that way. External factors always change. Bringing in new leaders or employees will change the dynamics, the economic environment, employment rates, etc., and change how you and your team function. Stresses and strains of current business problems may drive decisions with knock-on impacts that contradict the norms of your company culture. Be considerate of what this means in the short and long term. What are you willing to disrupt, and for the sake of what?

---·⚡·---

Chapter Eight:
Environmental Force

O ur environmental force is about the physical placement and environment in which we live and work. There's a connection between the other five forces, but most strongly with our social force. Our preferred personal characteristics and how we thrive or stumble in certain social settings, dictate the environment and surroundings we are attracted to when choosing where to live or work.

Consider the environments that have made you feel most safe and welcome. You likely gravitate toward the familiar, where people have something in common with you. It stems from experience. If you were brought up in a certain part of the world and most people in that environment tend to remain there or close by, you may seek to do the same. You are familiar with the surroundings, how to get around, and where the best places to go are. You have built a community. When things this familiar feel this good, it can be hard to comprehend another way.

The age of travel has expanded our scope of community. We are intrigued to explore other environments, but for most, this stops at vacation or maybe a temporary work assignment relocation. How many times have you enjoyed a break either inside or outside of your country of origin and wondered at the sights in awe, but upon returning home, felt a comfort and ease that anchored you to appreciation with gratitude for what you have? You may order from your favorite restaurant or organize time with friends and family you have missed while being away. This is "home."

This feeling also transcends into the work environment. Leaders should recognize this dynamic when making intentional decisions on the work environment that best enables their humanforce. What decisions do you make where individuals and teams can work from that balances the organization's needs and provides an environment where individuals can thrive?

Through the COVID pandemic, we have seen so many swings in thinking around optimal working conditions. I'll be honest: I've always enjoyed the in-office experience, sidebar conversations in breakout areas, and office space that inspires and encourages collaboration. I was convinced that this was the best way to maximize the output of people's work.

This is true in certain trades and situations, but in many office environments, the pandemic forced us into a different routine. For many, our homes became our offices. How we engaged and collaborated across teams, and our industries changed.

This notion that we could not be as productive at home was proved wrong by many. I went from cynic to complete advocate for work-at-home policies for most positions. I had worked within a brick-and-mortar environment for over twenty years.

My time management, ability to focus on the most important things, limit distractions, and manage the conflicts I often felt between work and family improved vastly. All in all, my stress levels decreased. The conversations with my teams have become more meaningful rather than transactional. I now understand the forces at play with how our environment shapes our ability to function with greater or lesser energy to thrive.

Consider a recent or past change in your working environment. What were some of your emotions leading up to, during, and after the change? What was most challenging? What energized you? What was different about the sense of community? How did that impact you? What did you change? How did you adapt?

From all these questions, what did you learn? Answering and reflecting on these questions are helpful to you as a leader and your humanforce. Just because what you did in one environment led to success does not mean the same approach will work within the dynamics of a new environment and community. We must do our research, listen, learn, explore, design, and employ evolving skills and competencies that best meet the needs of delivering the results in a new environment and community of people.

In the movie *Shang-Chi and the Legend of the Ten Rings*, the story moves you through various locations. Each new location presents a choice for each character that transforms their thinking and embraces the environment's characteristics.

As we are introduced to Shang-Chi's parents, you expect to encounter a hostile situation, with his father intent on invading this small village called Ta Lo.

Ying Li and Yu WenWu, Shang-Chi's mother and father, begin to fight, but WenWu's strength is soon overpowered by the beauty of Ying Li's rhythmic energy. She is completely at one with her environment in nature, and, as such, at one with her assailant. Rather than fight against him, her movements seem to fold into his and lead them both into a powerful choreography of ethereal combat. The ease and grace by which she disarms WenWu's strikes are magical, just like the beauty surrounding them.

As their relationship develops, both Ying Li and WenWu renounce their past and give up their powers.

The blend of both pasts is merged in the home they build together; a home where they would raise their children and are surrounded by beauty and living a life of pure joy.

All this is cut short when tragedy befalls the family and Shang-Chi's mother is brutally murdered by his father's past enemies.

WenWu sets about rebuilding his army, intent to avenge the loss of his wife. Their once beautiful and peaceful home becomes a cold, uninviting prison for Shang-Chi and his sister. There is no love, only pain and suffering.

Shang-Chi runs away at age fourteen to escape his father's oppression, and his life becomes a series of avoidance and fear of anything of value or importance. He keeps his community to the very few he trusts. He lives in an old garage made into a one-bedroom apartment in walking distance to his parking attendant job. He is unwilling to commit to anything, significantly downplaying his physical and academic talents.

I can go on, but you get the point; each environment influenced a state of being for Shang-Chi and his family. They were still the same people, but environment and circumstance influenced their choices and created certain energy patterns that either helped or disabled their impact. The energy can be felt through the characters' connection with their different environments. When the environment is vibrant and thriving, so are they. When the environment is cold, destructive, and dysfunctional, so are they.

So, what environments fuel your energy, and which take your power elsewhere? Have you stopped to look around you and determine what this means to you?

Let's return to the notion around placement I introduced at the beginning of this section. Your choices or circumstances that have you placed in a particular situation are significant sources of energy lifts or drains. How easy or hard is it for you to do what you must do each day? The simplest things can make a massive difference.

For instance, if you work from home but your internet connection is poor, you will face multiple challenges in completing your work each day. Each event is an opportunity for stress and reduced productivity. If you work in an office, how easy or hard is it to get to and from work each day? Is the commute long and expensive? This can put strain on your finances and energy reserves by the time you get to work or return home.

Maybe your commute is reliant on public transportation, so when the bus, train, or plane is late or cancelled even, this can put additional strain and stress into your schedule. This all takes energy, and as we've discovered in earlier chapters, our energy is precious. We need to know how to pivot in the moment to maximize our energy in any given challenge, but if that challenge is a daily business as usual drain, this is not sustainable for the perfectly imperfect hero leader. You need to reconsider your environment and how it best serves you or not.

Your home, local conveniences, available resources, work environment, proximity to friends and family all make a difference. The difference they make depends on what uniquely best serves you and those close to you—your community. From there you are much better positioned to do your best work as a leader.

Exercise: Exploring Environmental Energizers and Drainers

As leaders, it is crucial to understand what energizes and drains us within our community and work environment. This exercise will help you gain clarity on the factors that contribute to your energy levels, allowing you to optimize your performance and well-being.

1. Reflect on Energizing Moments:
Take a moment to reflect on times when you felt energized and motivated within your community or work environment. Consider the following questions:
- What specific activities or tasks made you feel excited and engaged?
- Were there any particular interactions or collaborations that left you feeling inspired?
- Did any specific aspects of the environment or community contribute to your sense of energy and enthusiasm?

2. Identify Draining Factors:
Now, shift your focus to moments when you felt drained or depleted within your community or work environment. Ask yourself:
- What activities or tasks tend to drain your energy and motivation?
- Are there any specific interactions or relationships that leave you feeling drained?
- Are there aspects of the environment or community that contribute to your sense of exhaustion or disengagement?

3. Analyze Patterns:
Look for patterns and commonalities in your reflections. Are there specific themes or recurring factors that consistently energize or drain you? Consider the following aspects:
- Types of tasks or projects
- Interactions with specific individuals or groups
- Environmental or community factors

4. Create an Energizers and Drainers List:
Based on your reflections and analysis, create a list of your personal energizers and drainers. This list will serve as a reference point for future decision-making and self-care. Be as specific as possible, noting the activities, people, and environmental factors that contribute to your energy levels.

5. Take Action:
Now that you have identified your energizers and drainers, it's time to take action. Consider the following steps:
- Maximize energizers: Find ways to incorporate more of your energizers into your daily routine or work tasks. Seek opportunities to engage in activities and communities that align with your passions and strengths.
- Minimize drainers: Explore strategies to minimize or mitigate the impact of your drainers. This could involve setting boundaries, delegating tasks, or seeking support from colleagues or mentors.
- Communicate your needs: Share your insights with other leaders, your team or community, expressing how certain

activities or factors impact your energy levels. This will help foster a supportive and understanding environment.

Remember, self-awareness is key to optimizing your performance and well-being as a leader. By understanding what energizes and drains, you can make intentional choices that align with your values and contribute to your overall success and fulfillment.

Take the time to regularly revisit and update your energizers and drainers list, as your needs and circumstances may evolve over time. Embrace this exercise as a tool for self-care and personal growth, allowing you to lead with authenticity and vitality.

It doesn't stop there, though. All that you have applied to maximize your environmental energy force holds true for those who work for you. Your humanforce. Every business decision you make on the environment and culture you set for your humanforce has a direct relationship toward how you enable and power their energy to do their best work for themselves, your customers, you, and your company. And, yes, there is no such thing as one size fits all.

Each group, department, or set of individuals may need something different to balance their energy forces optimally for life and work. Your decisions and the tone you set is vitally important. Know that if your personal preference is to be in-office and collaborating in person, this sets the tone for others that this is an expectation that they, too, work from the office. That might not be how you get the best of them, though, so be open and considerate to others' unique needs. If you want to maximize your human force, you need to really listen, understand, and make the necessary calls to serve the majority and be prepared to adapt around the edges.

Leadership is not straightforward. You will continually be challenged to make decisions, and that will require you to make choices. That doesn't mean it's an either-or situation. Research shows that the most effective leaders are those who can make decisions and lead with a both/and mindset.

If you reflect on the story of Shang-Chi's parents, they both came from different backgrounds and experiences. They didn't choose to fully conform to each other's ways; they instead chose a path that worked for both to have the best life together. They both relinquished power to gain something that was even more powerful, empowering, and fulfilling.

This brings me to another challenge. How do you enable the power of diverse talents and provide an environment where all can thrive? Surely, they each need surroundings conducive to optimized productivity. This is where we come back to blending the energy sources on your Quinjet. Each of the five energy forces need to be in balance, and that will mean something different when applied to you as an individual and how you lead your teams and how you lead your organization. However, the questions you ask are very similar:

Individual	Team	Organization
What's my purpose?	What's my team's purpose?	What's the purpose of the organization?
What goals do I have?	What are the most important goals for my team?	What goals are important for my organization?
What does success look like for me?	What are the measures of success for my team?	What does success look like for the organization?
What do I need to be successful?	What does my team need to be successful?	What does the organization need to be successful?
How do I best optimize my strengths?	How can I optimize the combined strength of my team?	How can I optimize the value the organization provides to our customers?
What needs to be true for me to perform at my best?	What needs to be true for my team to deliver for our customers?	What needs to be true for the organization to deliver differentiated value to our customers?
What's my why?	What's my team's vision?	What's the vision and mission that drives this organization?

While the scale of impact is different, the decisions you make as a leader are closely tied to the variation of possible outcomes at different scales. My research points to balancing where standardization is necessary to build trust, safety, and security, while also providing an appropriate level of flexibility to key areas that matter to your humanforce.

For example, if the standard protocol is for productive collaboration between the hours of 11a.m. and 3p.m. each weekday, and the need for in-person collaboration through structured ceremonies are core to about 40 percent of the roles in a particular organization, you will make decisions on what buildings, resources, facilities will be most helpful to those endeavors. At the same time, you know some people may be unable to attend in person, and to ensure the ability for all to thrive, you invest in conferencing technology and virtual collaboration tools to amplify collaboration for a hybrid of in office and virtual engagement model.

Further flexibility may be provided when considering hiring decisions. If you have invested in enabling a humanforce that can thrive in a hybrid collaboration environment, then it will be less necessary to restrict which footprints you are willing to seek candidates from. This can also have the further benefit of enabling superior talent to what may be available in your brick-and-mortar environment and provide opportunity for increased diversity of talent.

If, on the other hand, the type of work conducted within your organization requires in-person presence to deliver a particular service, you may not have that flexibility. Instead, you may look at flexibility in other forms, such as shift options; transportation ease; on-site facilities that extend a service toward better living (subsidized grocery prices with free delivery services to homes, subsidized on-site childcare, or healthcare facilities). The type and size of your organization will dictate what options are available to you, but in all cases the consideration of how you balance standardization and flexibility for the betterment of helping your humanforce thrive in their working environment is vitally important.

Choosing What, When, and Where?

The perfectly imperfect hero leader is highly attuned to how a particular setting can either amplify or destroy a message. It's important to consider the placement of any messaging within the environment that best suits the occasion.

Let's take an example: You are about to deliver a particularly difficult message to a colleague. You know that the message will land hard on them because your observations will open them up to a blind spot that is getting in the way of moving an important agenda forward. It's important to you that they trust you and know you are on their side. You want to ensure the message is heard clearly and that it prompts discovery on how to move forward. You want to avoid judgment, accusatory language, and curb the potential for defensive or argumentative behavior from your colleague.

You consider the sensitivity of the conversation, the message you want to deliver, and the outcomes you desire. As you fully consider all options, you can now decide when, how, and where this conversation will be had.

I'm not going to prescribe a set of rules, because the outcome depends on the situation and relationships ahead of this conversation, which will dictate the environment you choose to set up to have a constructive outcome. However, it's fair to say that this should not be a conversation held in public or in a group environment. It also would serve to have an inviting and open setting, but at the same time private. It would be fitting to ensure no barriers or direct face-to-face positioning in the environment chosen.

The important takeaway is that it's not enough for the perfectly imperfect leader to make do with what their environment allows for. They are intentional and deliberate in their choices of environment to conduct their most important conversations, decisions, and presentations.

I want to share a particular preference of mine when I want to spur creativity or engage in a thought partnership to a particularly challenging problem. I have found that the best way to have these conversations is outside or in an open setting that is inviting but less structured than a meeting room or in front of a whiteboard. These situations are mainly for one-to-one or very small group settings and involves walking. The act of walking inspires energy. The picturesque surroundings inspire openness, mindful thinking, and creativity. The lack of formality allows for a sense of safety, with the unspoken rule of "anything goes;" "no idea is a bad idea."

I also notice that I choose this environment when I want to provide observations from which I want others to act on. The environment is calming, and walking seems to energize people with a willingness to accept an observation without judgment and move to action with increased ease and acceptance. What makes the difference is that when walking, you naturally are side by side. There is not this feeling that your reactions and body language are being analyzed when receiving feedback. It provides room for the recipient to absorb the words and think, without having to feel the pressure of an immediate response.

Post the 2020 pandemic, I am finding myself needing to rethink and relearn this concept now that we are having more in-person interactions. I've noticed that when looking for a forum for collaboration, I rely on my admin to choose the right type of room for the meeting without providing instruction on what I want. As a result, there are times when the layout of the room doesn't aid the type of conversation I want to have. There's an awkwardness in the flow of the material and engagement of the participants.

When your environment is ill matched to the purpose of the engagement you are hoping for, it can have a dramatic impact on how you show up, how others engage, and how well you achieve your desired outcomes. The mood and energy of the room can either serve you or not, and that has everything to do with how you set up the environment to drive toward the desired outcome. It's all about deliberate and intentional placement of what is needed to enable you and others to thrive.

What's the "Sense" in All This?

I turn attention next to the power of the five senses and what this means for environmental energy. Smell, sounds, touch, taste, and vision all play an important role in this part of the energy force. While this seems obvious, personal association to these senses can make or break a person's day and land differently for each individual. The smell of freshly baked bread can bring comfort to one person and evoke fear for another.

Consider the first individual has positive memories associated with the smell of bread. It reminds them of joyful times growing up. The family would gather around and savor the delicious taste of their father's freshly cooked bread devoured alongside other foods that left them full, satisfied, and content.

Another person may associate the smell with a violent encounter on their way home from school. When the bullies left him crying outside the back of the local bakery, the smell of bread always takes him back to that moment of fear and loneliness.

These are two different responses to the same stimuli. One is disempowering and the other is empowering. Even so, there is an element of judgment that can be applied here. In most circumstances, the smell of freshly cooked bread summons a positive response. If the purpose of the business you are running is to create comfort and satisfaction, you may choose to fill the air with a scent that most commonly is associated with positive outcomes or influences a specific reaction. It's worth doing your research first to ensure you get it "mostly" right.

Sound can be a big enabler or detractor in the work environment. Most office spaces tend to favor an open plan, although research suggests that most office workers are more productive in environments that are less distracting, mainly as it relates to sound but also visually.

This is one I struggle with a lot. I love being around people; it gives me energy and invites healthier habits for taking breaks and collaboration. However, when my day is full of meetings with others across different footprints or requires heads-down work for addressing emails or finishing up a presentation, I find it super hard to concentrate in an open-plan office. I become conscious of how loudly I may be talking and keep adjusting and scanning my surroundings for reactions. This is distracting to the work I need to get done, or I may engage less effectively in an attempt to overcorrect. Equally, I can find myself getting frustrated by the interruptions of chatter around me or the conversation of a loud talker adjacent to me. All in all, I get less done and I find myself in a state of frustration. Clearly, I am not doing my best work.

Do not underestimate the power of the working environment you set for your people. Consider carefully the positioning of the building, what is available in the surrounding areas, the ease of access to the building and other resources, the colors on the walls and furniture, the texture of the furniture, the positioning of the windows in relation to workstations, the amount of light, ability to control the intensity of the light, the soundproofing of meeting-room walls, the visibility into an office space, the expanse of space or confinement required. It's a lot to consider, but depending on what work you intend to get done in the space you provide your people, these decisions are extremely important.

If, like me, you also have a home office, deciding which room, where to face the desk, what artwork is hung on the walls, and what bookshelves are available has played a big part in my effective and productive days. I have adapted the space over time and found some areas to be far too cluttered, which becomes mental clutter if I leave it too long to purge or rearrange. You know instantly if the space you work in gives you the right level of energy you need to be at your best. Take time to be in the space and reflect on your achievements and energy levels each day. What do you notice? What's working? What isn't working? What needs changing? And then do it. Make the necessary changes. You deserve to do your best work every day and live a joyful life. So, make it a priority to check your environment and create a routine to adapt based on what you notice.

Optimizing Teams for Peak Performance: The Role of Environment, Resources, and Technology

Organizations strive to optimize their teams to achieve peak performance in today's fast-paced and competitive world. Extensive research has been conducted to understand how the environment, resources, and technology can be leveraged to create an atmosphere conducive to teams doing their best work. This section of the book aims to summarize key findings from this research, highlighting strategies that can enhance team productivity, collaboration, and overall success.

Creating an Enabling Environment:
Research consistently emphasizes the importance of a supportive and empowering environment for team optimization. Key factors include:

1. Psychological Safety: Teams thrive in an environment where members feel safe to express ideas, take risks, and learn from failures without fear of judgment or retribution. Leaders should foster an atmosphere of trust, open communication, and respect. We explored this in more detail in the section on Cultural Force. Revisit that section to remind yourself of the interconnectivity to environmental forces.

2. Clear Goals and Roles: Clearly defined goals and roles provide teams with a sense of purpose and direction. When team members understand their responsibilities and how they contribute to the objectives, they are more likely to be motivated and engaged. Revisit the earlier sections on motivation and engagement to better explore how this all intersects.

3. Collaboration and Communication: Encouraging collaboration and effective communication channels is vital. Teams should have opportunities for regular interaction, knowledge sharing, and brainstorming sessions to foster creativity and innovation. Determining what environment you create for your organization and teams is critical to driving successful outcomes.

Optimizing Resources:
Providing teams with the necessary resources is crucial for their success. Research highlights the following aspects:

1. Adequate Time and Workload Management: Teams need sufficient time to plan, execute, and reflect on their work. Leaders should ensure realistic deadlines and workload distribution to prevent burnout and maintain productivity. This is also important to drive resilience when challenges arise, and the stakes are high. You can provide all the skills required to manage stressful situations. Still, if you fail to provide the foundational space in their working schedule to use those skills constructively, you create an environment left to chance in succeeding on the other side of the challenge.

2. Skill Development and Training: Investing in continuous learning and skill development enhances team members' capabilities and confidence. Providing training opportunities and access to relevant resources equips teams to tackle challenges effectively. An environment that encourages and empowers continual growth and learning leads to more productive and successful teams.

3. Access to Information and Expertise: Teams should have easy access to relevant information, data, and subject matter experts. This enables informed decision-making, problem-solving, and promotes a culture of knowledge sharing. Consider how you provide this access with ease to all.

Leveraging Technology:
Technology plays a pivotal role in optimizing a team's performance. When the environment you set for people to do their best work optimizes technology at its core, you enable a team to smash through the ceiling of stretch targets. Key considerations include:

1. Collaboration Tools: utilizing digital platforms and tools that facilitate seamless collaboration, such as project management software, virtual meeting platforms, and shared document repositories, enhances communication and coordination among team members.

2. Automation and Efficiency: Leveraging technology to automate repetitive tasks and streamline processes frees up time

for teams to focus on higher-value activities. This can include using workflow management systems, AI-powered tools, or task automation software.

3. Remote Work Capabilities: In today's evolving work landscape, providing teams with the necessary technology and infrastructure to work remotely is essential. This includes secure remote access, virtual communication tools, and cloud-based platforms for seamless collaboration.

Optimizing teams for peak performance requires a holistic approach that considers the environment in relation to the resources and technology provided. Creating an enabling environment that fosters psychological safety, clear goals, and effective communication is foundational. Equipping teams with the necessary resources, including time management, skill development, and access to information, enhances their capabilities. Lastly, leveraging technology, such as collaboration tools, automation, and remote work capabilities, empowers teams to work efficiently and effectively.

By implementing these strategies based on research findings, organizations can create an environment where teams thrive, leading to increased productivity, innovation, and overall success. Continuous evaluation and adaptation to evolving needs will ensure teams remain optimized for ongoing success in a dynamic and ever-changing business landscape.

Insights—What Did You Learn?

- Environmental energy force is about the placement and environment in which we live and work.
- We are attracted to the familiar.
- Our past environment influences our choices of where to live and work.
- The need for familiarity, safety, and trust in our surroundings transcends into the workplace.
- We do our best work when we feel secure, safe, and trusting of our environment.
- Consider which environment fuels your energy and which drains you. Apply this same consideration to those you lead.
- Your preferences may not be what works for your humanforce.
- Consider what work environments to standardize and which to balance flexibility for diverse talents to thrive.
- There is no such thing as one size fits all.
- Misplacement of the best-suited environment for your engagements will lead to impeded outcomes.
- Be deliberate in choosing when and where you engage with others to best deliver desired outcomes.
- Make "sense" of your space to gain the energy to thrive each day.

---·⚡·---

Chapter Nine:
The Finale: Get Ready for Takeoff

Here you are in the final chapter of this book. This exploratory journey to find the perfectly imperfect hero leader within serves as the catalyst of insights that will power you toward your leadership legacy.

Your leadership legacy is one that only you can uniquely curate and it starts with connection and relatability to yourself first. What makes you, *you*, creates the best leader you can be. It's the ingredient that so many of us miss tapping into, especially in our early careers. We are so consumed by the pace of change around us that we naturally get swept up in the waves placed in our path.

The energy forces that fuel your leadership Quinjet will shift out of balance as you hit turbulence, take hits, experience energy drains, find energy surges in one or two engines. These external factors will always be present to test our resolve, presenting new opportunities for lessons to be learned.

Intentional focus, effort, and practice to maintain optimal performance is necessary. That's your foundation. When you can master that, you create the power to lead at new altitudes where the energy you leave behind can be consumed and optimized by others in ways you could never have imagined. The power of your leadership legacy has just reached outer space.

In case you haven't already done so, I want to provide one last exercise designed to help leaders connect with their past experiences and clarify their purpose, values, and mission in life. By reflecting on significant moments and lessons from the past, leaders can uncover valuable insights that guide their decision-making and shape their personal and professional journey. Be honest with yourself and step out of your comfort level of thinking purely about surface-level experiences, but go deep and surface those stories that you have likely buried away from conscious thought.

1. Set the Stage:

Find a quiet and comfortable space where you can reflect without distractions. Have a journal, a blank sheet of paper, and a pen ready to record your thoughts and reflections. Try to use drawings and symbols that can connect with emotions and feelings as you put pen to paper.

2. Journey Through Significant Life Experiences:

Close your eyes and take a few deep breaths to center yourself. Begin to mentally journey through your life, recalling significant experiences that have shaped you. These experiences can be personal, professional, or a combination of both. Visualize what that journey may look like from where you were sitting in your Quinjet. Where did you lose altitude, what knocks did you take, where did you rise and glide? What obstacles did you encounter? What did you notice about the decisions you made? Consider the following prompts:

- Think about a time when you felt a deep sense of fulfillment and purpose. What were you doing? Who was with you? What help did you get? What feelings and sensations do you recall? What values were you embodying during that experience?
- Reflect on challenging situations or obstacles you encountered. What do you notice about when and how you overcame them? What stands out to you about those times? What emotions and self-talk do you remember? How useful were the words you heard from others and spoke to yourself? What strengths and values did you rely on to navigate through it?
- Recall a moment when you positively impacted someone's life or in your community. What values were at the core of that action?
- Consider any transformative or pivotal moments that shifted your perspective or led to personal growth. What did you learn from those experiences?

3. Identify Common Themes and Values:

Review your reflections and look for common themes, values, or patterns that emerge from your past experiences. Pay attention to recurring values, passions, or missions that have guided your actions and decisions. Write them down in your journal or on a sheet of paper.

4. Craft Your Purpose Statement:

Based on the themes and values you have identified, begin crafting a purpose statement that encapsulates your mission in life. This statement should reflect your core values and the impact you aspire to make. It can be a concise sentence or a paragraph. Take your time to refine and articulate your purpose statement, ensuring it resonates deeply with you.

5. Reflect and Align:

Take a moment to reflect on your purpose statement. Does it align with your current beliefs, aspirations, and goals? Consider how it can guide your decision-making, actions, and leadership style. Reflect on how living in alignment with your purpose can bring fulfillment and meaning to your personal and professional life.

6. Commitment and Action:

Make a commitment to yourself to live in alignment with your purpose, values, and mission. Identify specific actions or behaviors you can incorporate daily to honor your purpose. These can be small steps that gradually align your actions with your values and mission.

Conclusion:

By connecting with past experiences and reflecting on the values and lessons they hold, leaders can gain clarity about their purpose, values, and mission in life. This exercise serves as a guide to help leaders uncover their authentic selves and align their actions with their deepest aspirations. Embrace this exercise as a tool for self-discovery and commit to living a purpose-driven life that positively impacts both yourself and those around you.

Rising Above the Clouds

What does it take to sustain, persist, and rise above the clouds that want to pull you down? Here's what I discovered:

It's your unshakable belief in your purpose, values, and mission in life. Discovering what that is will evolve over time and become clearer the more you challenge yourself to connect and relate to what makes you who you are. Many call it vulnerability or living your truth. We can find what they are when we make space to listen to our thoughts and feelings, apply deep introspection, and evolve our perspectives.

Often, what we think or feel in any situation can be seen as inappropriate or less constructive to verbalize in a business or social setting, and that is often true. So, we instead suppress or ignore it to move forward.

What incredible leaders do is find the avenues, tools, and resources to address those thoughts and feelings and lean into deeper discovery that brings connection and relatability to their purpose, value, and mission. From there they can use that data to transform their thinking and evolve their ability to act with constructive optimism, allowing them to arrive at more productive solutions and decisions. It's a constant growth circle:

The Growth Circle

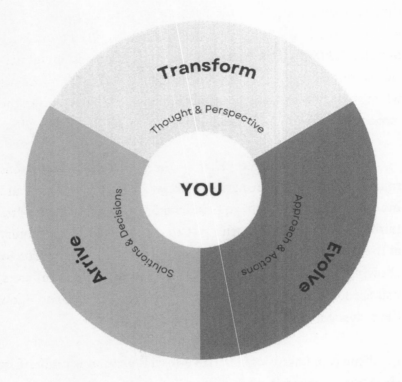

We introduced tools and resources you can use to practice centering back to your clarity of purpose in the Mental Force chapter of this book, using the DoorS methodology. I can't express enough how vital it is to regularly revisit and practice this methodology for sustained resilience to your ever-evolving goals and decisions.

Extraordinary leadership is not a destination that you reach and then maintain. It's a practice that has its ups and downs.

You are constantly learning, changing, adapting. You have a curiosity that powers you to revolve around the growth circle, time and time again, gaining something new each time. You do your best work on the other side of standing on the blunt edge of potential failure. You push the boundaries with meticulously carved out energy reserves, preserved for the precise moments when you know you need to apply a surge of energy to make the impossible possible.

I like to represent our energy reserves as a cup that needs space to fill when we are at the height of achievement. Those are moments to be prepared for. If our cup is already full of other less fulfilling stuff, we have nothing left to secure total achievement at the exact time we need it. We, in effect, leave it to chance by allowing things to uncontrollably spill over. In those moments, you are less able to retain what you need in the cup and allow the riches you need to spill over.

This is precisely why I place so much emphasis on the first stage of the DoorS methodology. You need to always create and preserve space in your cup by disconnecting your mind and body to rest and be present in calm. Your Quinjet will serve you so much better in the precise moments that matter most when you have allowed it to power down and rest.

When the inevitable knocks are felt, and the storms hit, your practice of being present and sitting in the calm will be your best friend, allowing you to approach actions and decisions with thoughtful and deliberate clarity. While the frenzy builds in the actions of others, you can focus with increased clarity and identify the clearings and best path forward more so than others. You also can lead with a calming influence and guide that clarity in others. Don't underestimate the power of this first step in the DoorS methodology.

Illustration by Taina Layla Cunion

Don't stop there, though. There is always a layer in that cup that takes up space of things that don't serve you well. Get rid of it. Take time to figure out what tasks, habits, thoughts are no longer serving you and stop doing them. They take up too much of your precious energy.

The space that you now have at the top of that cup is pure amplified energy that can take your biggest achievements to a whole new level. Add to that all the goodness in the bottom of the cup and your Quinjet is ready to fly anywhere, anytime.

Here's a quick reminder of what's below surface level in your cup. It's where your past achievements and most treasured moments reside. It holds your inspiration council, who can always be called on when you are seeking truth and the courage to open up to new possibilities. This constant practice of reminding yourself what you have already accomplished and expanding your capacity to think bigger and broader provides the momentum you need to tune in to and invite opportunity.

This foundation of a growth mindset allows you to explore and funnel where you want to redirect your attention and energy, helping you craft your next steps to new goals. Once you reach clarity, you can step forward through the doorway that leads to a big or small set intention. Remember, the key here is not to just set the goal but to establish the confidence and self-belief that you will succeed. Keep this up front and center in your mind even in those moments when you're not consciously thinking about what you are aiming for. Your internal robotic processing automation system, your subconscious, will kick in and influence how you show up, what choice you make, where and with whom you leave an impression that attracts the means by which you can achieve what you have set out to accomplish.

Why is this last part so very important? Because perfectly imperfect hero leaders use that self-belief to find a path beyond the failed attempts, barriers, and obstacles that present. It's that unshakable commitment to succeed in what is most important to them. They will naturally use their time and energy wisely and find it easier to say "no" when something might get in the way of progress toward that destination. It's easier for them to tune out the noise and negative energy that might surround them. Their self-talk is much kinder and rational.

That last part is important—rational thinking. Why? Because this doesn't mean that they blindly forge forward to succeed at all costs. Not at all. They will build community that not only supports them but will challenge and point out blind spots. They will deeply listen, engage, trust, and verify. They are super grateful and humbled by those who courageously speak up with sound reasoning. Ego is put to the side and curiosity and generosity rises.

I encourage you to take a moment and consider everything you have read and what's popping for you in this final chapter. Let me help you get started:

1. There is no such thing as the perfect leader.
2. Great leaders are always practicing, adapting, and learning—curiosity rules.

3. Find your unique leadership power—it's the sum of everything you are and have been and aspire to be.
4. True, deep connection to self and others is key.
5. There is humility in how extraordinary leaders relate to others and how that connects to their purpose, values, and mission in life.
6. Great leaders' goals transcend what they alone can make possible. What they go after serves a bigger, more meaningful purpose that others can take and grow to be even more than they had imagined.
7. What extraordinary leaders inspire is contagious. They are the catalyst that sparks a movement.
8. Great leaders protect their time to focus on what matters most and leave space to amplify that power reserve when they need it most.
9. The perfectly imperfect hero leader has unshakable commitment to their purpose, values, and mission in life.

So, what now? How well-balanced are your Quinjet's energy forces? Where are you taking these insights? What's your flight plan toward your leadership legacy? Well, that's yours to write. I have created space for you to take the pen and get started.

Think of this last chapter less about ending this book, but more about you starting the first chapter of your own leadership legacy story. There is a perfectly imperfect hero leader inside you waiting to rise. It's time to thrive at warp speed and venture into outer space. Now, you are powered up to lead like never before. Get ready for takeoff!

My Leadership Legacy Story

_____

_____

_____

_____

_____

_____

_____

_____

_____

_____

_____

_____

_____

_____

_____

_____

_____

_____

_____

_____

_____

_____

_____

_____

_____

Reference list

Breus, Dr. Michael. 2022. "National Sleep Day" article. May 18, 2022. Sleepdoctor

Briggs, 2022. Myers Briggs Test. Excerpts are taken directly from the report of test results for Marisa Thomas (Author) 2022.

Cambridge English Dictionary, 2023. Definition of "Shine". https://dictionary.cambridge.org/us/dictionary/english/shine

Cherry, Heather. 2021. "The benefits of resting and how to unplug in a busy world." Article published by Forbes. January 15. https://www.forbes.com/sites/womensmedia/2021/01/15/the-benefits-of-resting-and-how-to-unplug-in-a-busy-world/?sh=ce11f3121338).)

Clifton, 2022. Clifton StrengthsFinder assessment results for Marisa Thomas 2022.

Cohen, Adam. 2022. Leadership Insights. Interview by Marisa Thomas. June 28, 2022. 02:42. 10:51

Dispenza, Joe. 2020. "Breaking the Habit of Being Yourself." Audible released March 26, 2020, Encephalon LLC, Chapter 1. Chapter 4. Accompanying PDF with Audible, Figure 5A narrative.

Hogan, Blake. 2022. Leadership Insights. Interview by Marisa Thomas. June 16, 2022. 08:30. 13:41

https://www.google.com/search?q=Definision+of+value

James, LeBron. 2020. Opening remarks to "Train your Mind - Vol 1." Calm App

Larson, Jeremy D. 2019. "Why Do We Obsess Over What's 'Relatable'?" New York Times. January 8. https://www.nytimes.com/2019/01/08/magazine/the-scourge-of-relatable-in-art-and-politics.html

Lord, Robert. 2022. Leadership Insights. Interview by Marisa Thomas. June 24, 2022. 08:13

Miller, Donald. 2017. "Building a StoryBrand." HarperCollins Leadership. Audible version.

Morris, Nigel. 2022. Bank On It podcast. "Founding Fintech - Episode 2 - From Capital One to QED Investors." Interview by John Siracusa, July 19. 2022. Listen Deck.

Morris, Nigel. 2022. Leadership Insights. Interview by Marisa Thomas. September 22, 2022. 23:39. 24:47. 26:52. 27:44.

Ox Science. 2023. "Difference between Matter and Energy." https://oxscience.com/matter-and-energy/

Oxford Languages. 2023. Definition of the word "Value".

Oxford Languages. 2023. Definition of the word "relate".

https://www.google.com/search?q=definition+of+relate

Pacheco, Danielle; Singh, Dr Abhinav. 2023. "Why do we need sleep." Article published by the Sleep Foundation. Nov 3. 2023. https://www.sleepfoundation.org/how-sleep-works/why-do-we-need-sleep

Simmons, Jemma. Marvel character. Agents of S.H.I.E.L.D. 2020 Netflix TV series. "The steps you take don't have to be big. They just need to take you in the right direction." Multiple episodes.

The Flash. 2022. Netflix, July 7. 2022. "You can read minds. I can think in superspeed." Series 8 - episode 1.

VIA, 2005. Values in Action Assessment. Positive psychology page of the University of Pennsylvania. Excerpt from Marisa Thomas's (authors) own top five results from her 2019 assessment) https://ppc.sas.upenn.edu/resources/questionnaires-researchers/survey-character-strengths